Chesapeake Bay

Waterside Dining Guide

WHITEY SCHMIDT

MARIAN ★ HARTNETT
PRESS

The Chesapeake Bay Regions

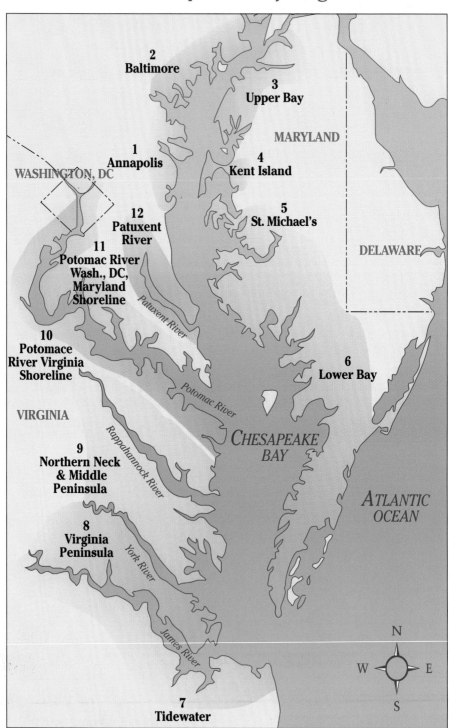

Movable Feast

Chesapeake Bay, Chesapeake free.
    It's plenty of seafood for you and me.

You can have New York and all its glitter.
    Give me the shore and an oyster fritter.

Take a walk on a rickety pier,
    Then sit by the window and drink a beer

Harbor front road, Bay Creek back.
    Catch a view of a lone skipjack.

I don't want capers or liver paté,
    Give me some crabs steamed in Old Bay.

Fresh shucked oysters, Smithfield hams,
    Oyster Rockefeller, and Casino Clams.

Corn-on-the-cob and sliced tomatoes,
    Fresh shore peaches, and home-fry potatoes.

Maryland crab soup, vegetable style,
    And hot steamed oysters heaped in a pile.

So come by air, come by sloop,
    Come and try the cream crab soup.

Come and try the fresh sea trout.
    The good food is what it's all about.

You can drive around or sail across.
    Bring the wife or bring the boss.

Come try what the good cook bakes.
    Enjoy the taste of Virginia crab cakes.

Forget the Mac and Quarter Pounder.
    Savor the taste of fresh baked flounder.

Fix your face, take a powder,
    then try a bowl of fresh clam chowder.

She crab soup is hot and cheery.
    Try a bowl topped with sherry.

Broiled bluefish makes a great filet.
    Try some for dinner to brighten your day.

Watch for ducks up in the sky,
    And look on the menu for oyster pie.

Chincoteague oysters with Tabasco sauce,
    Soft-shell crabs are worth the cost.

You can charter a boat, round a crew,
    head on out for oyster stew.

Do they have steamed clams? Take a few.
    Just get a table with a water view.

For Susie

Printed in the
United States of America
First Printing 1997
ISBN 0-9613008-9-2

Library of Congress Catalog Number 97-73247
Copyright © 1997 by Marian Hartnett Press
Box 88
Crisfield, Maryland 21817

Contents

How to Use This Book

For the purpose of this book, the Chesapeake Bay is divided into twelve geographical regions. There is something for everyone—from the excitement of major cities to the scenic calm of tiny towns and quiet backwaters. The choice is yours.

Maps: On page ii is a map of the entire Chesapeake Bay area showing the twelve regions covered in this book. At the beginning of each regional section is a detailed map showing the location of each restaurant in that section.

Restaurant Information: For each restaurant, I've listed name, address, phone number, business season, hours, waterfront location, credit cards accepted, and house specialties. In addition, symbols indicate the general ambiance of the establishment, whether reservations are recommended, whether there's a place to dock your boat, the availability of outdoor dining, whether the restaurant serves steamed crabs, and the availability of handicap access. Naturally, all of these are subject to change, so it's a good idea to plan ahead and inquire by telephone. That way, you can be assured of having a seat by the window when you arrive!

Restaurant Descriptions: Many of these restaurants are well-known; others are remote and secluded. The format offers a brief note on each restaurant's history, decor, and other features. The intent is not to compare the quality of one kitchen's crab soup with another's, but simply to point out some items I found especially appealing—whether a great view, terrific food, or a unique ambiance.

Credit Card Abbreviations

AE American Express	**MC** MasterCard
Disc Discover Card	**Visa** Visa
DC Diner's Club	

Symbols

 Steamed crabs   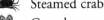 Outdoor dining

Casual atmosphere   Full bar

Upscale atmosphere   Dockage

Romantic atmosphere   Handicap access

Reservations recommended

Introduction

This book was written for residents, of or visitors to, the Chesapeake Bay area who love seafood and also love a good view of the water. One of the best places to find great seafood, naturally, is right on the coast, where skipjacks, trawlers, and crab boats come in daily with fresh catches, and it goes without saying that the coast is also the best place to find a wonderful water view! There is no better way to experience the full flavor of the Chesapeake Bay's history than to meander through the coastal towns, breathe the salt air, and steep yourself in the flavor of the past with a taste of today.

Chesapeake cookery offers endless opportunities for exploration and delight, and Chesapeake restaurants seem to have available an infinite variety of local fish, clams, oysters, crabs, mussels, scallops and shrimp, sometimes supplemented by fresh or frozen seafood from faraway places. The variety of offerings is widened by the fact that each can be fixed in any of a number of ways—poaching, steaming, braising, stewing, baking, broiling, grilling, smoking, sautéeing, stir frying, deep frying, or even raw on the half shell. The outstanding chefs of the Bay region, with their unique appetizers, soups, chowders, bisques, sandwiches, and entrées, know no culinary boundary.

On any given day, as the Bay sparkles under the bright sun, I can think of hundreds of restaurants where I could enjoy a festive meal and lazily gaze out at the glistening blue water. Let me unfold for you the secrets of a seasoned restaurant traveler. That's what this book is all about—sharing what I've learned about the region's restaurants with you. As a food critic and lifelong resident of the area, I've come to know and enjoy all 212 eating establishments included in this guide.

• Along the Eastern Bay near Grasonville, Maryland, there's the laid back **Upper Deck Restaurant**, where you can relax and enjoy an osprey's view of the watermen as they dock their workboats and harvest the day's catch.

• Or at **Hemingway's** in Stevensville, Maryland, you can watch countless sailboats glide past chugging barges and tugs before a Bay Bridge backdrop.

• Or you can spin down a dirt road to the secluded and rustic **Tim's Rivershore Crabhouse** south of Washington, DC in Dumfries, Virginia where you'll find brown butcher paper on the tables and mallets just waiting for you to stop by and start cracking those delicious steamed blue crabs.

Every one of the restaurants I've selected overlooks the Chesapeake Bay or one of its many rivers or tributaries. So whether you're a visitor or a resident, let me help you locate just what you had in mind—a great Bay restaurant with a great view.

1: About the Annapolis Area

This Chesapeake Bay area stretches for nearly 200 miles from its northern reaches in Maryland to where it joins the Atlantic Ocean off the southern coast of Virginia. It's surrounded by natural waterways and laced with rivers, creeks and inlets. We begin our dining guide in the tiny town of Chesapeake Beach, Maryland, located about 35 miles from Washington, DC and about 25 miles from Annapolis. Annapolis itself is considered by many as the sailing capital of the world and offers visitors to Chesapeake Bay recreation, entertainment and dining options too numerous to list.

Follow the simple map and restaurant descriptions in this chapter and prepare to dine your way through the area! Savor unusual combinations, discover secret recipes and techniques, soak up food history and lore, and treat your palate to the great authentic foods that the Annapolis area has to offer.

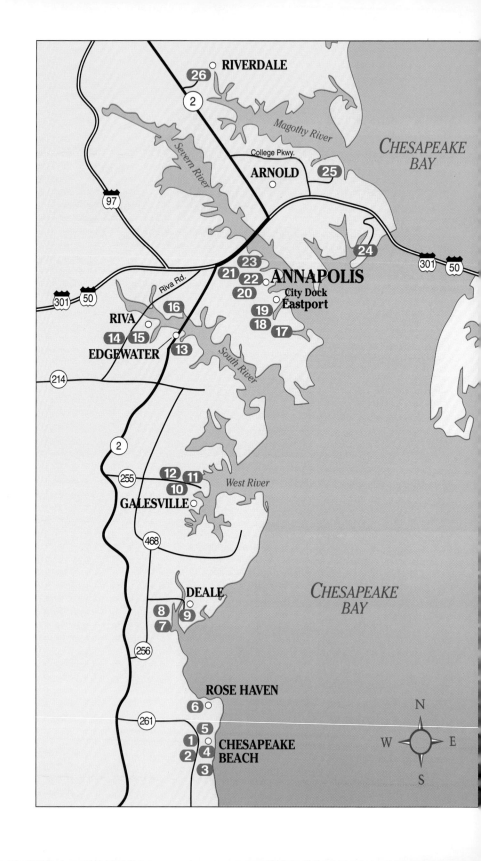

Annapolis Waterside Dining

INCLUDES: Chesapeake Beach, Rose Haven, Deale, Galesville, Edgewater, Riva, Annapolis, Arnold, and Riverdale, Maryland

1. Abner's Crab House
2. Vic's Italia by the Bay
3. Buckmaster Seafood
4. Rod 'n' Reel Restaurant
5. Smokey Joe's Grill
6. Herrington on the Bay
7. Bobby D's Chesapeake Grille
8. Happy Harbor Inn
9. Skipper's Pier
10. Topside Inn
11. Steamboat Landing
12. The Inn at Pirate's Cove
13. Surfside 7
14. Mike's Restaurant
15. Paul's on the South River
16. Fergie's Restaurant
17. Sam's Waterfront Café
18. Buddy's Crabs & Ribs
19. Middleton Tavern
20. Vespucci's Restaurant and Bistro
21. Pusser's Landing
22. Carrol's Creek Café
23. The Chart House
24. Cantler's Riverside Inn
25. Deep Creek Restaurant
26. Riverdale

❶

Abner's Crab House

3748 Harbor Road, Chesapeake Beach, Maryland
410-257-3689

BUSINESS SEASON: April through January
HOURS: open daily for lunch and dinner
WATERVIEW: Fishing Creek/Chesapeake Bay
CREDIT CARDS: MC, Visa
HOUSE SPECIALTIES: cream of crab soup, Maryland-style crab soup, oyster stew, steamed crabs, steamed seafood platter, crab cakes, steamed shrimp, stuffed shrimp, stuffed hard crab, broiled rockfish, New York strip steak

Abner's Crab House has been a Chesapeake Beach landmark since 1966. Bobby Abner is one of those rare entrepreneurs who not only cooks the crabs he serves, but goes out on the bay and catches them. Bobby's day begins long before most of ours, and he's still working when most of us are home sleeping. Abner's is a casual family-style crab house featuring a simple but varied menu at popular prices. Several dining room walls are decorated with murals of watermen at work on the Bay painted by local artist Virginia Akens.

Abner's is most famous for steamed crabs, but is also known for beer-steamed or spiced peel-and-eat shrimp. If you'd like to try a variety of tastes, try "Abner's Seafood Treat"—you'll get soft-shell crab, crab cake, fish, steamed and fried shrimp, and oysters—plus two vegetables.

❷
Vic's Italia by the Bay

3800 Harbor Road, Chesapeake Beach, Maryland
410-257-1601

BUSINESS SEASON: all year
HOURS: open Monday through Thursday for dinner only; Friday through Sunday for lunch and dinner
WATERVIEW: Fishing Creek/Chesapeake Bay
CREDIT CARDS: AE, DC, Disc, MC, Visa
HOUSE SPECIALTIES: Chesapeake Ravioli, wood-fired pizza, New England clam chowder, broiled scallops, fried calamari, filet of flounder, crab cakes, crab imperial

Pleasure-seekers preparing for a day at the beach are always concerned with finding good food and drink at a reasonable price. The solution is a visit to Vic's Italia by the Bay Cantina. Here two talented chefs produce some mighty good cooking. Vic Daddi and Bil Shockley combine their culinary skills to present a menu that offers special, unique dishes but does not overwhelm the diner with too many offerings.

Chesapeake Ravioli—freshly made pasta stuffed with local crab meat and served in a light cream sauce—is one dish you'll want to try. On Fridays and Sundays, Vic's serves an excellent prime rib, and on any night of the week, be sure to savor the flavor from Italy's finest wood-burning pizza oven. My favorite is the Salciccia—Italian sausage and pepperoni over a fresh plum tomato sauce. Mmmm!

Buckmaster Seafood

Mears Avenue, Chesapeake Beach, Maryland
301-855-7239

BUSINESS SEASON: April to November

HOURS: open Tuesday through Sunday for lunch and dinner

WATERVIEW: Fishing Creek/Chesapeake Bay

CREDIT CARDS: MC, Visa

HOUSE SPECIALTIES: steamed crabs, corn on the cob, steamed clams, fresh fish, fresh
   soft-shell crab, crab meat, oysters, snow crab legs

Chesapeake Beach was named and incorporated by the Maryland Assembly in 1894
and became a bustling resort in the early 1900s. Back in those days, a building lot
with a waterveiw could cost as much as $300! One of the greatest attractions at the
beach was salt water bathing. Today few people bathe in the Bay, but they *do* visit
the Chesapeake Beach Water park. Here you can rent a tube and slide, slide, slide.
It's a family-friendly place suited for all ages.

   Another family-friendly place is Buckmaster Seafood, located adjacent to the water
park. Strictly open-air dining presents a problem on rainy days, but if the skies are
sunny, this crab house and carryout is the place to be. Operated by Sue, Graham,
Greg and Grady Buckmaster, this 60-plus year old family business specializes in steamed
crabs and other local seafood—freshly caught by one of the three G's.

④

Rod 'n' Reel Restaurant

Mears Avenue, Chesapeake Beach, Maryland
410-257-2735

BUSINESS SEASON: all year
HOURS: open daily
WATERVIEW: Chesapeake Bay
CREDIT CARDS: AE, Disc, MC, Visa
HOUSE SPECIALTIES: crab cakes, crab imperial, stuffed rockfish, fried oysters, soft-shell crabs, artichoke crab dip, broiled or stuffed lobster tail, shrimp 'n' crab cake, steak 'n' crab cake, Mariner's Feast, Shrimp Trio

From 1898 to 1935, city dwellers in Washington, DC and Baltimore flocked to Chesapeake Beach by railroad and steamer for summer fun in the luxurious resort town. The railway station is now a museum, and the town is best appreciated for its fishing fleet, shops, water park and seafood restaurants.

Located adjacent to the museum is the Rod 'n' Reel Restaurant, with its sport fishing fleet lining the docks. The mid-Bay area produces rockfish, bluefish, trout, drum, spot, croakers, Spanish mackerel and perch. The Rod 'n' Reel is a great place to try the rockfish. Maryland's state fish can be yours fileted and broiled or fried, and it can be stuffed with classic crab imperial. A recent addition to the Rod 'n' Reel menu that's sure to please shrimp fans is the Shrimp Trio, which includes shrimp fried and roasted as well as shrimp scampi.

⑤
Smokey Joe's Grill

Mears Avenue, Chesapeake Beach, Maryland
410-257-2427

BUSINESS SEASON: all year

HOURS: open daily for lunch and dinner

WATERVIEW: Fishing Creek/Chesapeake Bay

CREDIT CARDS: AE, MC, Visa

HOUSE SPECIALTIES: barbecued baby back ribs and chicken, grilled garlic shrimp kabob, combination platters, crab cakes, aged black Angus sirloin, grilled tuna, grilled swordfish, barbecued beans

"Smokey Joe" was the nickname of Gordon Stinnett (1924-1993), the son of local entrepreneur Wesley Stinnett and Elizabeth Stinnett. Nicknamed Smokey Joe by his World War II buddies in Europe, he had a fishing boat constructed by the famous Chesapeake boat builder Bronza Parks of Wingate, Maryland upon his return from the war. The "Little Smokey" was 50 feet long and ran head boat and private charters until it was deemed too small for the heyday of the "hard head" fishing of the time. In 1958, Gordon contracted with Paul Jones to build the Smokey Joe II. "Big Smokey" was 65 feet long and licensed for 90 passengers—the biggest fishing boat to hit Chesapeake Beach!

Today you can sit by the windows of Smokey Joe's Grill and overlook the biggest charterboat fleet on the Chesapeake Bay … and while you're enjoying the view, remember where you are. This is the "reel" place for steaks, ribs, and chicken.

6

Herrington on the Bay

7149 Lake Shore Drive, Rose Haven, Maryland
410-741-5101

BUSINESS SEASON: all year

HOURS: summer: open for lunch and dinner; winter: dinner only

WATERVIEW: Herring Bay

CREDIT CARDS: AE, MC, Visa

HOUSE SPECIALTIES: Herrington's crab cakes, stuffed shrimp, lobster ravioli, scallop and lobster fettucini, lobster ravioli, avocado with imperial crab, award-winning crab soup, crab dip, Cajun shrimp, pasta St. Croix

Herrington Harbour South Marina Resort is located at the southernmost tip of Anne Arundel County. Exquisite sunsets abound, inviting romantic evenings on a beach that reminds one of the Bahamas, with its palm trees and shade cabañas. You'll enjoy viewing yachts moored in the quiet marina basin as you stroll picturesque cobbled walkways meandering through the area. (It won the 1996 Marina of the Year award.) Along these walkways you'll find a well-maintained kitchen garden from which Chef Amy Glaeser harvests fresh herbs for Herrington on the Bay.

Ask your server about Glaeser's fresh seafood creations, which include a special crab cake recipe using only the best Maryland crab meat and fresh herbs. One of my favorite dishes is the Rose Haven Chicken, marinated in fresh rosemary, homegrown "Rose Haven" garlic and virgin olive oil, and then perfectly chargrilled.

Photograph by Beverly Fuss

Bobby D's Chesapeake Grille

421 Deale Road, Deale, Maryland
410-867-0750

BUSINESS SEASON: all year

HOURS: open Monday through Friday for lunch and dinner; Saturday and Sunday for breakfast, lunch, and dinner

WATERVIEW: Tracy's Creek/Herring Bay

CREDIT CARDS: MC, Visa

HOUSE SPECIALTIES: steamed crabs, spiced shrimp, Maryland crab soup, hot crab dip, prime rib au jus, garlic steak, chicken primavera, grilled salmon primavera, Cajun catfish

Deale, Maryland is a tiny hamlet with old-time family values and an easy-going lifestyle. Twenty-five miles from Washington, DC and 20 miles from downtown Annapolis, it's a haven for boating, crabbing and fishing. If you come to Bobby D's by boat, ease into Rockhold Creek in Deale and turn left into Tracy's Creek. Just before the bridge you'll find Bobby D's sprawling Chesapeake Grille, offering casual dining indoors and out. The Tiki Bar has plenty of picnic tables for cocktails, snacks, and spicy steamed crabs. Inside are a bar, a sports room, and several dining areas with great views.

Hot crab dip is a dish I can't pass up at Bobby D's. This divine recipe is a creamy casserole of backfin crab meat with cheddar and cream cheese. And owner Bobby Durbin says, "My Maryland crab cakes are second to none"—prepared daily with fresh all-backfin crab meat (95% crab meat). Try one and see what you think!

8

Happy Harbor Inn

533 Deale Road, Deale, Maryland
410-867-0949

BUSINESS SEASON: all year
HOURS: open daily for breakfast, lunch, and dinner
WATERVIEW: Rockhold Creek/Herring Bay
CREDIT CARDS: Choice, Disc, MC, VISA
HOUSE SPECIALTIES: shrimp sampler platter, crab cakes, crab imperial, pan-fried
chicken, crab soup, weekly dinner specials, bucket of steamed clams, imperial
stuffed mushroom caps, clam chowder

Happy Harbor Inn, one of the Bay area's best-known restaurants, is located at the
foot of the Rockhold Creek bridge. Informal and unsophisticated, the purist gour-
mand may very well pass it by. But if you enjoy good home cooking in unpretentious
comfort, this should be your choice.

"Yes! We have crab soup!" says Happy Harbor's menu. I tried it and the clam chowder; both were good. Top notch crab cakes, too—enveloped in a dark crust with a
distinct peppery taste. Here's a sampling of Happy Harbor's popular weekly dinner
specials: prime rib, country seafood buffet, shrimp sampler platter (a dozen steamed
shrimp, shrimp salad, fried shrimp … shrimply delicious!). On Friday's it's the all-
you-can-eat Clamdigger Special—New England or Manhattan clam chowder, clams
(fried, raw, and steamed) and corn on the cob. Enjoy!

❾

Skipper's Pier

6158 Drum Point Road, Deale, Maryland
410-867-7110

BUSINESS SEASON: all year

HOURS: open daily for lunch and dinner

WATERVIEW: Rockhold Creek/Herring Bay

CREDIT CARDS: MC, Visa

HOUSE SPECIALTIES: steamed crabs, crab cake dinner, broiled salmon, Cajun grilled tuna steak, baby back ribs, Nana's meat loaf, fried shrimp dinner, Maryland crab vegetable soup, chargrilled chicken dinner

If you arrive by car, Skipper's Pier is at the very end of Drum Point Road. If you arrive by boat, the first things you'll notice as you enter Rockhold Creek are the two-story waterfront dock of Skipper's Pier bar and the Deale water taxi. The water taxi is informal and a lot of fun—step on board and travel as you please along the area's beautiful creeks. And Skipper's Pier is a great spot for watching boats, from 30-foot sloops to the working vessels that abound in this part of the Bay.

As you wait to be seated, you'll see what diners keep coming back for—heaping piles of hot steamed crabs seasoned with just the right amount of pepper to complement the crab meat's natural sweetness. You'll also want to try the crab cakes—either alone or in a sandwich—with tangy tartar sauce, french fries and a crisp garden salad. Still hungry? Take the water taxi to Bobby D's or Happy Harbor.

🔟

Topside Inn

1004 Galesville Road, Galesville, Maryland
410-867-1321

BUSINESS SEASON: all year
HOURS: open Wednesday and Thursday for dinner only; Friday through Sunday for
lunch and dinner; closed Monday and Tuesday
WATERVIEW: West River
CREDIT CARDS: AE, MC, Visa
HOUSE SPECIALTIES: Topside Platter, crab imperial, crab cakes, stuffed flounder, Italian
fare, shrimp and scallop tequila, prime rib, filet mignon, rotisserie chicken

As you drive down Galesville Road and reach the traffic signal at Route 468, you'll
notice the Quaker Burying Ground (established in 1672). Just beyond it is Tulip Hill,
a magnificent Georgian mansion built in 1752 and a landmark to steer upon for captains seeking the channel of the West River. It's here on the waterfront adjacent to
the public pier that you'll discover the Topside Inn.

The Topside isn't fancy, but over the years it's developed a pleasant personality. The
upstairs outdoor balcony from which it gets its name only has nine tables, so plan ahead
if this is your choice. The downstairs dining room has a convivial atmosphere with
dark beams, polished brass and a view of the water across the road. The menu abounds
with dishes from the land and sea including Italian food. Wednesday night the special is pasta; Thursday spiced shrimp; and Friday, Saturday and Sunday's it's chef's choice.

Steamboat Landing Restaurant

4851 Riverside Drive, Galesville, Maryland
410-956-6200

BUSINESS SEASON: all year

HOURS: open Wednesday through Friday for dinner only; Saturday and Sunday for lunch and dinner

WATERVIEW: West River

CREDIT CARDS: AE, MC, Visa

HOUSE SPECIALTIES: seafood sauté, rack of lamb, classic Caesar salad, Steamboat crab cakes, broiled rockfish, seared tuna, California rolls, Angus beef, Tuscan shrimp

Owner Larry Policano bought Steamboat Landing in 1995 and renovated it in style. You'll find custom-cut Italian granite, Honduran mahogany woodwork, soft lighting, brass fixtures, and a menu to rival any in the world. A wide range of dishes includes Policano family recipe Italian meatballs and certified Angus beef as well as gourmet seafood dishes like sautéed Tuscan shrimp: fresh Gulf shrimp sautéed in olive oil with fresh garlic and plum tomatoes, served in a nest of angel hair pasta.

The "New Steamboat" bar, as you might expect, offers a variety of draft beers; house wines are served by the glass or bottle.

A little history: The restaurant is built on pilings from a landing first used to dock steamboats from all over the world when the Annapolis harbor was full. It is surrounded by water … a perfect setting for a perfect meal.

The Inn at Pirate's Cove

4817 Riverside Drive, Galesville, Maryland
410-867-2300

BUSINESS SEASON: all year
HOURS: open daily for lunch and dinner
WATERVIEW: West River
CREDIT CARDS: AE, DC, MC, Visa
HOUSE SPECIALTIES: smoked bluefish, baked oyster sampler, hot mariner's platter, flounder longhorn, crab dip, oyster pan roast, cream of crab soup, broiled seafood platter, filet mignon with béarnaise sauce, Veal Oscar

The tiny town of Galesville is located about 20 miles south of Annapolis. Although it has but one traffic light, it has three restaurants within a 5-minute walk of one another. The Inn at Pirate's Cove is built on the site of an old oyster house that was turned into a restaurant in the 1920s. In the early 1980s, present owner Bob Platt took over, and he's responsible for the waterfront lounge and two large dining rooms.

On the dinner menu a smoked bluefish appetizer was one of the best I've ever tasted. The firm filet, smoked with a hint of cracked pepper, was served with horseradish cream sauce and crackers. For oyster lovers, the baked oyster sampler will definitely please: barbecued oysters, Oysters Rockefeller, and cove oysters topped with crab imperial. The Inn's cream of crab soup is a carefully guarded recipe they've served for the last 30 years. And there's much more … seafood fettucini … flounder longhorn … you can't go wrong.

⑬

Surfside 7

48 South River Road, Edgewater, Maryland
410-956-8075

BUSINESS SEASON: all year
HOURS: open daily for lunch and dinner
WATERVIEW: South River
CREDIT CARDS: AE, MC, Visa
HOUSE SPECIALTIES: Clams Casino, steamed shrimp, steamed crabs, grilled salmon
salad, spicy shrimp pasta, filet mignon, prime rib, Maryland crab cakes, soft-shell
crabs, deep fried shrimp, fish of the day

Surfside 7 is on the south side of the South River at the foot of the Route 2 Bridge.
Over the years the building has had numerous occupants, and present owners Jerry
Osuna and Robin Nye and chef John Rudolph have taken great steps to make it a
very friendly place.

In season, you'll enjoy eating on one of the decks—a casual setting for enjoying
seafood, raw bar, sandwiches, spicy steamed shrimp, and crab soup. On several vis-
its, I've been impressed by the crab soup, steamed shrimp and Maryland crab cakes,
which were all lump backfin—your choice, fried or broiled. Dinners come with homemade lime tartar sauce, Creole mustard, baked potato and vegetable du jour. Every
meal is accompanied by warm, friendly service and scenic charm. The popularity of
Surfside 7 with locals and visitors alike is proof of its success.

14

Mike's Restaurant

3030 Riva Road, Riva, Maryland
410-956-2784

BUSINESS SEASON: all year
HOURS: open daily for lunch and dinner
WATERVIEW: South River
CREDIT CARDS: AE, MC, Visa
HOUSE SPECIALTIES: steamed crabs, stuffed flounder imperial, baby back ribs, lobster
   tail, crab cakes, soft crabs, combination seafood platter, fried oysters, broiled
   scallops, broiled orange roughy

The menu at Mike's is broad, offering steaks and baby back ribs, Alaskan red salmon, and broiled catfish—although many come here just to eat steamed crabs. Salads, are impressive, especially the Greek—a meal in itself.

But let's not get away from the crabs! Mike's is a popular spot Monday through Friday for an all-you-can-eat crab feast. Be aware that the crabs are all cooked at one time, so if you fancy the feast, plan to get there when they come off the heat. Don't get me wrong—I like crabs hot or cold, any size with any amount of seasoning, but the best are those just pulled from the water and popped into the pot. To assure that yours are freshly steamed, do as I do and have them cooked to order—but keep in mind that this takes about 20 minutes, so you'll be forced to while away the time with a pitcher of beer and the view of the beautiful South River in all its splendor!

Paul's on the South River

3027 Riva Road, Riva, Maryland
410-956-3410

BUSINESS SEASON: all year

HOURS: open daily for lunch and dinner

WATERVIEW: South River

CREDIT CARDS: AE, MC, Visa

HOUSE SPECIALTIES: soup sampler, steamed clams, oysters, mussels, crab imperial, pastas, chateaubriand, fish of the day, t-bone steak, filet mignon, broiled seafood array, stuffed oysters, lobster tail, roasted tenderloin of lamb

Ψ ♥ Υ ⚓ ♿ ☎

This South River restaurant offers casual sophistication and beautiful sunsets to go with a continental cuisine. Paul's features exciting and innovative selections such as Petit Crab Imperial (prepared with lump crab meat, topped with imperial sauce and baked to a golden brown); coconut shrimp (dipped in coconut flour and deep fried—I've tasted none better); and steamed mussels (12 Maine mussels topped with a watercress pesto sauce). Then there are old dishes with a twist—like the Chateaubriand made with tuna! You can have traditional Chateaubriand as well, and both are served with a salad, potatoes, vegetables and béarnaise sauce. You'll also be impressed with Paul's little extras like hot-from-the-oven chewy dinner rolls and a carafe of wine kept cold at tableside. Suffice it to say that anything you order at Paul's will be good regional fare prepared and served with style and culinary skill close to genius.

Fergie's Restaurant

2840 Solomons Island Road, Edgewater, Maryland
410-956-8075

BUSINESS SEASON: all year

HOURS: open daily for lunch and dinner

WATERVIEW: South River

CREDIT CARDS: AE, DC, Disc, MC, Visa

HOUSE SPECIALTIES: corn and crab chowder, French onion soup, roasted prime rib, grilled filet mignon, veal Norfolk, pork chops, chicken marsala, lobster tail and filet mignon, seafood and pastas, stuffed shrimp, Fergie's famous crab cakes

You don't have to wait for a special occasion to have an exceptional meal at Fergie's. I wish I could eat here every day! With a unique location overlooking the South River, Fergie's has had several names and owners over the past 10 years, but Gonzalo Fernandez has come home to run it as it should be run. Formerly maitre d' at the Maryland Inn's Treaty of Paris Restaurant, he's also the co-founder of Northwoods, a highly acclaimed Annapolis eatery.

No matter where you sit, you'll have a magnificent view of the water while you enjoy a glass of wine and a wonderful array of appetizers (you could make a meal of them; my choices would be escargots, hickory shrimp and mushrooms Rockefeller). The soups and entrées are also first-rate, and a nice touch is the Sundowner menu—dine before 7 PM on weekdays and 6 PM on weekends and pay reduced prices.

17

Sam's Waterfront Café

2020 Chesapeake Harbour Drive, Annapolis, Maryland
410-263-3600

BUSINESS SEASON: all year; closed Mondays during winter
HOURS: open daily for lunch and dinner
WATERVIEW: Chesapeake Harbour/Chesapeake Bay
CREDIT CARDS: AE, MC, Visa
HOUSE SPECIALTIES: oyster chowder, shrimp tempura, caramelized sea scallops, grilled Atlantic salmon, grilled duck breast, sautéed rockfish, mixed seafood sampler, file mignon, sautéed shrimp with leeks, shellfish chowder

Ask any restaurateur what the three main ingredients of a successful business are, and the answer will be "location, location, location." At Sam's Waterfront Café, the three main ingredients are Mary Randall (owner), Richard Miletich (manager), and Philip Sokolowski (executive chef). Together they create a sophisticated staff whose forte is keeping flavors simple, yet expanding upon the Chesapeake cuisine. The restaurant's design will remind you of one of the Bay's old spider-type lighthouses. Inside it's light and airy, with huge windows.

On a recent visit I chose oyster chowder with applewood-smoked bacon and corn followed by an entrée of baked oysters served on a bed of crispy fried spinach and topped with butter-wine sauce, fresh breadcrumbs and crunchy pine nuts. I've judged many cooking contests over the years, and this dish was truly a winner.

18

Buddy's Crabs & Ribs

100 Main Street, Annapolis, Maryland
410-626-1100

BUSINESS SEASON: all year
HOURS: open daily for lunch and dinner
WATERVIEW: Spa Creek/Severn River
CREDIT CARDS: AE, DC, Disc, MC, Visa
HOUSE SPECIALTIES: steamed crabs, grilled red snapper, grilled shrimp, Buddy's
  seafood sampler, Maryland crab soup, crab cakes, soft crabs, snow crab, garlic crab,
  barbecued baby back ribs, broiled stuffed shrimp

The best advice for a visitor to Annapolis is to park the car and walk—up one side
of Main Street, around State Circle, and back down the other side. Once you're back
at the city dock, climb to the second floor and join the crowd at Buddy's Crabs &
Ribs. Buddy's has one of the best views in Annapolis, with huge windows all around
and marvelous views of the city dock and the pleasure boat traffic in "Ego Alley."

Buddy's is famous for its ribs, cooked until the meat falls off the bone and covered with a delicious sweet/tart/smoky sauce. But the star of Buddy's menu is the hard
shell blue crab. Its preparation is a ritual: crabs are layered in a pot of vinegar water,
covered with a mixture of salt, pepper, ginger, mustard, and who knows what else,
and steamed just long enough for the shells to turn an appetizing fiery red. Is your
mouth watering yet? At Buddy's the 20-minute cooking time will be worth the wait.

⑲
Middleton Tavern

2 Market Space, Annapolis, Maryland
410-263-3323

BUSINESS SEASON: all year
HOURS: open daily for lunch and dinner
WATERVIEW: Spa Creek/Severn River
CREDIT CARDS: AE, Disc, MC, Visa
HOUSE SPECIALTIES: award-winning Maryland crab soup, oysters on the half shell, steamed oysters, oysters Rockefeller, smoked fish of the day, hot crab dip, grilled shrimp, fresh baked garlic bread, crab Middleton, crab cakes, rockfish, lobster tail

From the Middleton Tavern menu: "An 18th century tavern was much more than a place to lodge and dine. The tavern served as a communication network long before there was the six o'clock news. ... news from far away was carried via the mariners who docked, dined, and boarded there ... [and] the tavern was a leading source of commercial enterprise as well. ... Taverns were also important to the social structure of the day ..."

Today a great way to begin a meal at Middleton's is with the house specialty—the oyster shooter. The "shooter" is a plump, robust oyster, topped with a sauce of horseradish, ketchup, Tabasco and vodka. It's served with a side glass of beer. The idea is to toss 'em down—they say "first fright, then delight." You'll enjoy Middleton's, its history, charm and food make it an enjoyable place to dine.

20

Vespucci's Restaurant & Bistro

87 Prince George Street, Annapolis, Maryland
410-571-0100

BUSINESS SEASON: all year

HOURS: open daily for lunch and dinner

WATERVIEW: Spa Creek/Severn River

CREDIT CARDS: AE, DC, Disc, MC, Visa

HOUSE SPECIALTIES: grilled filet mignon with a basil sauce, salmon with black olives and capers, grilled jumbo shrimp, grouper with associated seafood, Maine lobster, red snapper, chicken breast stuffed with meat, Tradizionale Maryland crab cakes

Vespucci's, a large glassed-in structure at the end of the dock, is the newest eatery to enhance the Annapolis waterfront. Located in what was the Harbor House, it's been extensively renovated and is now three restaurants in one, each with its own menu, kitchen and chef.

Upstairs is the Flagship, an elegant room featuring superb food served with an Italian flair. Downstairs is the Bistro, with a nice bar and several secluded eating spots where the pasta of the day is popular. And then there's my favorite place to dine—the open-air terrace. Give me a glass of chianti and I can dream hours away there. But man cannot live on wine alone, so last time I was there I tried the Gamberoni Amerigo: jumbo shrimp studded with Maryland crab meat, laced with garlic and herbs, and topped with a white wine and lemon sauce. Magnifico!

21

Pusser's Landing

80 Compromise Street, Annapolis, Maryland
410-626-0004

BUSINESS SEASON: all year

HOURS: open daily for breakfast, lunch, and dinner

WATERVIEW: Spa Creek/Severn River

CREDIT CARDS: AE, CB, DC, Disc, MC, Visa

HOUSE SPECIALTIES: jerk tuna, Cumberland sausage, chicken tropicale, old English fish & chips, Irish lamb stew, Chesapeake seafood pie, shepherd's pie, baked bayside rockfish, crab cakes

Spa Creek is the focal point of Annapolis; its mouth is Annapolis Harbor, and both sides of the creek are lined with hundreds of boats. "Ego Alley" is at the end of Spa Creek, and that's where you'll find the city dock, where all boaters that cruise the creek must turn around and head out. If you're ready to eat (and if there's room), tie up at Pusser's Landing at the Annapolis Marriott Waterfront. Inside, its elegant nautical theme complements the view of the sail and work boats that line the city dock.

The origin of the name Pusser is a corruption of the word "purser" that's been used by sailors for hundreds of years. Pusser's is also the name of a famous Caribbean rum, and at Pusser's Landing you'll enjoy a variety of rum drinks as well as Caribbean-style food.

22

Carrol's Creek Café

410 Severn Avenue, Annapolis, Maryland
410-263-8102

BUSINESS SEASON: all year
HOURS: open daily for lunch and dinner
WATERVIEW: Spa Creek/Severn River
CREDIT CARDS: AE, DC, MC, Visa
HOUSE SPECIALTIES: oysters Veracruz, shrimp and salmon empanadas, seared duck
  breast, Maryland crab soup, red wine onion soup, pistachio crusted catfish, shrimp
  and scallops tequila, Maryland crab cakes, prime rib, roasted free-range chicken

Carrol's Creek Café, on the Eastport side of Spa Creek in the Annapolis City Marina, has a sweeping panoramic view that includes the spire of St. Mary's Church, the Eastport bridge, the Naval Academy, the Colonial State house, and the hundreds of sailboats that line the Harbor. It's from this perspective that you'll understand why Annapolis is called the "Sailing Capital of the World."

On Sunday mornings, the dining room features a magnificent buffet—some say the best on the east coast. Also good (but not on the buffet) is the Carrol's Creek Chesapeake Bay Dinner. This signature dish begins with Maryland cream of crab soup and American Field salad (a crisp assortment of greens with raspberry vinaigrette) followed by expertly prepared baked rockfish and your choice of many desserts. A special treat is the chef's homemade New York cheesecake.

(23)

The Chart House

300 Second Street, Annapolis, Maryland
410-268-7166

BUSINESS SEASON: all year

HOURS: open Monday through Saturday for dinner only; Sunday for lunch and dinner

WATERVIEW: Spa Creek/Severn River

CREDIT CARDS: AE, Disc, DC, MC, Visa

HOUSE SPECIALTIES: Caribbean black bean soup, oysters on the half shell, cream of crab soup, Maryland crab soup, Maryland crab cakes, cowboy steak, rack of lamb, orange basil salmon, lobster pot pie, Chesapeake rockfish

The Chart House story began in Aspen, Colorado, where Buzzy Bent and Joey Cabbel, world-class surfers with an equally strong passion for skiing, launched the first Chart House. More than 30 years later, that first restaurant has grown into a chain of 60. Spectacular locations and unique historical buildings are a part of the Chart House style, and the Annapolis restaurant is no exception. Once home of the John Trumpy & Sons Boatyard (well-known during World War II as a builder of Navy war vessels), it retains the high ceiling and vast open-beam construction of that earlier business and houses an extensive collection of model ships, nautical scenes and historic Annapolis memorabilia.

The food lives up to its surroundings. Try the orange basil salmon, Maryland crab cakes, lobster pot pie, or New England lobster, and you won't be disappointed.

(24)

Cantler's Riverside Inn

458 Forest Beach Road, Annapolis, Maryland
410-757-1467

BUSINESS SEASON: all year
HOURS: open daily for lunch and dinner
WATERVIEW: Mill Creek/Chesapeake Bay
CREDIT CARDS: AE, MC, Visa
HOUSE SPECIALTIES: Captain Lou's seafood platter, soft crabs, steamed crabs, crab
   soup, crab dip, fried oysters, stuffed rockfish, crab cakes, Jimmy's steamed seafood
   platter, Cantler's scallop sauté, oysters on the half shell

Cantler's is one of the best and most popular restaurants on the East Coast, and one
reason for this is that it's truly a family business. With 18 kids in the family, there's
a brother, sister, son or daughter working in every phase of the operation. Jimmy Cantler,
the ninth child born to the Cantler family, bought the restaurant in 1974 and has
turned the once-average restaurant into one of the better eating establishments in the
country. Cantler's sits at the end of the Broadneck Peninsula at the end of a dead-
end street and looks out over Mill Creek and Martins Cove. Once you find your way
here, you may have to wait for a place to park. Inside, you'll find a dark, somewhat
rugged atmosphere with rows of long wooden tables. Blackboards are neatly lettered
with the day's menu. I'd recommend the steamed crabs if you're out to savor the flavor of the Chesapeake Bay—you'll be in for a treat.

Deep Creek Restaurant

1050 Deep Creek Avenue, Arnold, Maryland
410-974-1408

BUSINESS SEASON: all year
HOURS: open daily for lunch and dinner
WATERVIEW: Deep Creek/Magothy River
CREDIT CARDS: AE, Disc, DC, MC, Visa
HOUSE SPECIALTIES: crab cakes, deep-fried lobster tail, black Angus New York strip, baked salmon strudel, seafood penne, twin filet of beef, jambalaya, baked crab meat imperial, stuffed lobster, sautéed shrimp and scallops

Deep Creek is the first creek to port as you enter the mouth of the Magothy River at the southern tip of Gibson Island. Deep Creek Marina (formerly Captain Clyde's Marina) is on the north shore of the creek off the Magothy, and it's here you'll find the Deep Creek Restaurant.

This once was home port for some of the skipjack fleet during their winter oyster dredging, but the oysters I sought, I didn't find on my last visit. I *did* find delicious appetizers such as clams on the half shell, a steamed sampler of shrimp, clams and mussels). Salad entrées include Cobb, Caesar, spinach and shrimp. Signature dishes include Chef Keith Davis' own crab cake recipe: a 7-ounce portion of lump crab meat blend you can order broiled or sautéed. Another truly delightful selection is baked salmon strudel: salmon, spinach, artichoke hearts and boursin cheese wrapped in phyllo dough.

Chef Keith Davis

26

Riverdale Restaurant

143 Inverness Road, Riverdale, Maryland
410-647-9830

BUSINESS SEASON: all year
HOURS: open daily for lunch and dinner
WATERVIEW: Magothy River
CREDIT CARDS: Disc, MC, Visa
HOUSE SPECIALTIES: choice t-bone, fried oysters, combination platters: Buoy #9 (three
fried shrimp and a crab cake), The Riverdale (stuffed shrimp, soft crab, crab cake),
Marylander (crab cake and fried chicken), Count's Cove (soft crab and filet mignon)

The Magothy River has a unique charm, and its compact and cozy anchorage is shel-
tered from strong winds and boat wakes—an interesting stopover for visiting boaters.

The Riverdale Restaurant sits on a wide, terraced lawn with many stately trees. A
sign fixed to the door proudly announces "Fried Oysters," and judging from diner's
facial expressions, this made lots of people happy. I was seated near a large window
overlooking the Magothy and appreciated once again what a beautiful area this is.
My waitress quickly brought my drink order and informed me: "We serve dinner at
lunch or lunch at dinner … but if you want what's good, order the fried oysters." She
didn't have to tell me twice—I couldn't resist, and the resulting dinner was memorable: eight plump, juicy, crisply fried oysters that had me wanting to order more …
so I did!

2: About the Baltimore Area

Baltimore's waterfront has been the lifeblood of the city for centuries. The town was established as a port and shipbuilding center and recently grew in yet another direction when Harborplace revitalized the inner city and became one of the East Coast's top tourist attractions.

Harborplace consists of two glass-enclosed two-story pavilions overlooking the Inner Harbor. They house purveyors of produce, crabs, meat and dairy foods as well as a variety of eating places and specialty shops. In both pavilions, restaurants and cafés with waterside terraces offer outstanding food and drink as well as exquisite views of the harbor. In the unique neighborhoods and tiny bayside towns surrounding Baltimore are more interesting waterside restaurants, and those in this chapter are among the best—in quality, ambiance, service and value.

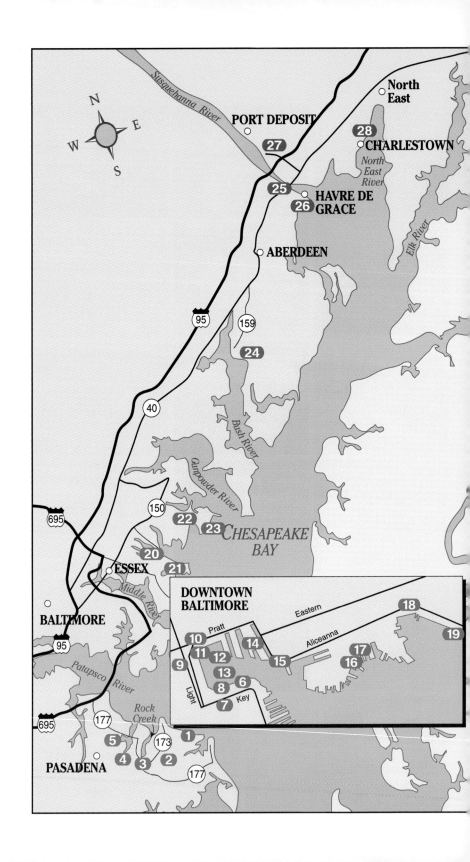

Baltimore Waterside Dining

INCLUDES: Pasadena, Baltimore, Essex, Aberdeen, Havre de Grace, Port Deposit, Charlestown

1. Nabbs Creek Café
2. Clark's Bayside Inn
3. The Cheshire Crab
4. Anchor Inn
5. Windows on the Bay
6. Pier 500 Restaurant
7. Joy America Café
8. Rusty Scupper
9. Berry and Elliot's
10. Windows Restaurant
11. Phillips Harborplace
12. Paolo's Restaurant
13. City Lights
14. The Chart House
15. Victor's Café
16. Lista's
17. Piccolo's
18. SS Captain James Restaurant
19. Bay Café
20. River Watch
21. Driftwood Inn
22. Decoys Seafood Restaurant
23. Wild Duck Café
24. Gabler's Shore Restaurant
25. Tidewater Grille
26. MacGregor's Restaurant
27. Tome's Landing
28. Wellwood of Charlestown

❶
Nabbs Creek Café

864 Nabbs Creek Road, Pasadena, Maryland
410-437-0400

BUSINESS SEASON: all year
HOURS: open daily for lunch and dinner
WATERVIEW: Nabbs Creek/Patapsco River
CREDIT CARDS: AE, MC, Visa
HOUSE SPECIALTIES: crab soup, crab cakes, seafood bisane, Captain's Delight (a pail of
    king crab, shrimp, scallops, mussels, corn on the cob, and potatoes—steamed
    Chesapeake-style), catch of the day, veal Oscar, chicken Chesapeake, seafood pie

Most of Nabbs Creek has fairly high banks lined with attractive homes. One, a large A-frame, overlooks Maurgale Marina and is the home of the Nabbs Creek Café. Owners Tony Listorti and Joe Avarino exude warmth and friendliness like 'Cheers'—and indeed, on my first visit, I was the only diner they didn't know by name! A large horseshoe-shaped bar takes up much of the indoor dining area, and two porches are perfect spots to enjoy your meal. On the recommendation of one of the regulars, I ordered the hot crab pot and enjoyed this cheesy delight, served in a mini-boule with bread cubes. I followed this appetizer with a crab cake. It contained a hint of garlic, came on a freshly baked roll, and was served with seasoned curly fries and a pickle. The menu says, "It speaks for itself!" and I agree. P.S. Don't pass up the seafood pie.

②
Clark's Bayside Inn

2042 Knollview Drive, Pasadena, Maryland
410-437-5711

BUSINESS SEASON: all year
HOURS: open daily for lunch and dinner
WATERVIEW: Patapsco River/Chesapeake Bay
CREDIT CARDS: AE, MC, Visa
HOUSE SPECIALTIES: seafood platter, broiled lobster tail, stuffed flounder, golden fried shrimp, broiled scallops, blackened tuna steak, fried oysters, Maryland crab cake platter, soft crab platter, steamed crabs

The Port of Baltimore is busier today than it was in the heyday of the clipper ships. One of the best places to watch the action is from the deck at Clark's Bayside Inn, where you'll enjoy a scenic panorama of the Patapsco River at its widest—about five and a half miles.

My favorite indoor spot is a dining room full of windows that overlook the Patapsco. Clark's appetizer menu is comprehensive, but I passed up the zucchini and mozzarella sticks in favor of clams casino, stuffed mushroom caps and Maryland-style crab soup. Entrées are generous and imaginative: try Clarke's Favorite—a New York strip steak smothered with large shrimp, fresh mushrooms and red bell peppers in the chef's special sauce. I also found the soft crab platter outstanding, and steamed crabs are available in season.

The Cheshire Crab

1701 Poplar Ridge Road, Pasadena, Maryland
410-360-2220

BUSINESS SEASON: all year

HOURS: open daily for lunch and dinner

WATERVIEW: Bodkin Creek/Patapsco River

CREDIT CARDS: AE, DC, Disc, MC, Visa

HOUSE SPECIALTIES: smoked fish platter, steamed crabs, crab meat cocktail, oysters
Rockefeller, Cheshire spiced shrimp, crab soup, Cheshire crab cakes, Skipjack stew,
broiled seafood platter, grilled New York strip

Like the grinning cheshire cat in Lewis Carroll's *Alice's Adventures in Wonderland*, you'll be grinning, too, when you discover the Cheshire Crab, located on beautiful Bodkin Creek at the Pleasure Cove Marina. First you'll enjoy sampling the area's largest selection of microbrewed draft beer on a 300-seat waterfront deck. Next I suggest you try the raw bar, offering fresh bay oysters or cherrystone clams on the half shell or a hickory-smoked fish platter. The menu also lists a dozen hot appetizers and traditional American soups prepared in classic Maryland style.

But leave room for the main course! I recommend the Cheshire Crab steamed seafood dinner: a 1¼-pound lobster, a large crab, four shrimp, four mussels, two clams, two oysters, an ear of corn on the cob, and an abundance of roasted red potatoes! If you haven't had steamed crabs here yet, you're missing something special!

Anchor Inn

7617 Water Oak Point Road, Pasadena, Maryland
410-437-0696

BUSINESS SEASON: all year
HOURS: open daily for lunch and dinner
WATERVIEW: Rock Creek/Patapsco River
CREDIT CARDS: AE, Disc, MC, Visa
HOUSE SPECIALTIES: crab cakes, soft-shell crab sandwich, catch of the day, grilled
   chicken breast, New York strip, seafood platter, crab dip, steamed shrimp,
   steamed crabs

There's nothing fancy about the Anchor Inn or its surroundings. Unpretentious cottages line the narrow streets leading to the restaurant, and in fact, it looks like it could be a summer cottage itself, sitting at the edge of a gravel parking lot almost directly on the waters of Rock Creek. It's not fancy inside, either, but what *is* special is the great job owners Kelly Walter and Dave Peel have done since since buying the restaurant in April 1997. I've known this couple for some time and have great confidence in their expertise. On a recent visit my friend Susie and I feasted on crab balls, a house special. These deep-fried bite-size jewels of the Chesapeake Bay were not spicy, but light and flavorful. But the real reason to come here is the seafood gumbo, chock full of sausage, shrimp and spicy tomatoes.

⑤
Windows on the Bay

1402 Colony Road, Pasadena, Maryland
410-255-1413

BUSINESS SEASON: all year
HOURS: open daily for lunch and dinner
WATERVIEW: Rock Creek/Patapsco River
CREDIT CARDS: AE, MC, Visa
HOUSE SPECIALTIES: grilled oriental duck breast salad, grilled Norwegian salmon, grilled Atlantic tuna, crab cake platter, stuffed shrimp, rainbow trout, chicken Chesapeake, grilled sirloin and stuffed shrimp combo, Windows stuffed veal

Windows on the Bay, in the midst of busy Rock Creek Marina, offers a pleasing panorama of Chesapeake watercraft.

On my most recent visit, I got off to a good start with the Ultimate Seafood Sampler—big, fat barbecued oysters with a homemade sauce that complemented the flavor of the briny bivalves; clams casino; spiced shrimp; mini crab cakes; and crispy shaved onion rings. I washed it all down with a glass of Fumé-Chardonnay, Hedges. Entrées at Windows come with a vegetable medley of cauliflower, broccoli buds tossed with carrot and zucchini matchsticks and a delicious baked potato.

Make sure you leave room for something sweet after dinner—the Windows dessert tray is a work of art containing many mouth-watering choices!

Pier 500 Restaurant

500 Harbor View, Baltimore, Maryland
410-625-0500

BUSINESS SEASON: all year

HOURS: open daily for lunch and dinner

WATERVIEW: Inner Harbor/Patapsco River

CREDIT CARDS: AE, DC, Disc, MC, Visa

HOUSE SPECIALTIES: New England clam chowder, Maryland crab soup, smoked salmon, steamed clams, catfish with shrimp étouffée, Pier 500 bouillabaisse, flounder and fresh asparagus, Maryland crab cakes, sesame salmon, baked stuffed shrimp

♥ Ψ Υ ⚓ ♿ ☎

The Pier 500 Restaurant is a part of Harbor View, a multi-million dollar complex on Baltimore's Inner Harbor that includes luxury high-rises and a world-class marina. Pier 500's chef Rob Johns uses the finest quality seafood in his artfully prepared dishes.

Start with the bouillabaisse—thick, rich and as good as any in France. The oriental duck salad is another treat: slices of seared, marinated duck breast accompanied by Euro-mix greens and raspberry vinaigrette. A good entrée choice is the black Angus New York strip steak with fluted mushrooms Provençale. The menu lists many other imaginative dishes, which feature locally grown produce and freshly caught seafood. Try the jumbo soft crabs pan-fried with a splash of sherry and the fabulous lobster Thermidor—a whole Main lobster steamed, sautéed with mushrooms, deglazed with cognac, chablis and cream, put back in the shell and baked with Swiss cheese on top.

Joy America Café

800 Key Highway, Baltimore, Maryland
410-244-6500

BUSINESS SEASON: all year
HOURS: open daily for lunch and dinner
WATERVIEW: Inner Harbor/Patapsco River
CREDIT CARDS: AE, DC, MC, Visa
HOUSE SPECIALTIES: oak-roasted whole rack of lamb, cinnamon and chocolate grilled
    tenderloin of beef, wasabi grilled natural chicken, wild Maryland rockfish, seared
    yellow-eye snapper

If you're planning a trip to the Inner Harbor, be sure to allow enough time to see
the American Visionary Art Museum, a first-of-its-kind gallery dedicated to the creative invention, intuition and original works of imaginative untutored artists.

The Joy America Café perches above the Museum. If you're lucky, you'll be seated
at the giant crescent-shaped window framing a view of the Patapsco River.

Just as the artists combine unusual materials in their creations, chef Peter Zimmer
makes his dishes artistic joys to behold! The menu changes with the season, but here's
a sampling from summer: shrimp with pistachio dumplings and miso vinaigrette, rice
noodles and fresh pineapple syrup or wild Maryland rockfish with roasted pear coulis
and just-dug potatoes. Dessert? Try the white chocolate pistachio mousse with bitter
chocolate decadence and black plum ice cream. Pure joy!

Rusty Scupper

402 Key Highway, Baltimore, Maryland
410-727-3678

BUSINESS SEASON: all year
HOURS: open daily for lunch and dinner
WATERVIEW: Inner Harbor/Patapsco River
CREDIT CARDS: AE, Disc, DC, MC, Visa
HOUSE SPECIALTIES: fresh oysters, Inner Harbor platter, filet mignon, sliced smoked
  salmon, Maryland jumbo lump crab cakes, pot of steamed golden neck clams,
  seafood alfredo, Scupper seafood Newburg, rockfish dijonnaise

Your table is waiting, the view is amazing; it's time to leave for the Rusty Scupper. If you haven't been to the Scupper lately, you haven't been there at all. There's a terrific new chef, a fresh new decor, even fresher seafood, and hands-down, the most magnificent view in Baltimore.

Fresh fish means special selections at the Rusty Scupper, and the availability of all seafood is subject to the season, weather and fishing conditions. Your selection will be lightly seasoned and chargrilled. The grilled salmon Bermuda is served on a bed of braised Bermuda onion and topped with béarnaise sauce and jumbo lump crab meat. The Louisiana-style catfish is also fresh off the grill and topped with a spicy Creole sauce and Bay shrimp. All entrées are served with the chef's selection of accompaniment, a Scupper salad and freshly baked bread.

Berry and Elliott's

300 Light Street, Baltimore, Maryland
410-605-2835

BUSINESS SEASON: all year
HOURS: open daily for lunch and dinner
WATERVIEW: Inner Harbor/Patapsco River
CREDIT CARDS: AE, DC, Disc, MC, Visa
HOUSE SPECIALTIES: grilled New York sirloin, lobster varioli, Maryland crab cakes,
    rockfish chowder, grilled Portobello mushrooms with arugula and fresh herb
    polenta, caesar salad, maple barbecued salmon, linguine seafood risotto

My first impression of Berry and Elliott's was of two chefs schooled in culinary art
at the finest New York establishments. What I found out was that they owned a market on Light Street, on the property acquired by the Hyatt Regency.

High atop this 5 star hotel, its windows overlook the Inner Harbor, teeming with
tugs, water taxis and other commercial traffic. Chef William Brooks is a culinary artist
whose talents shine in seafood entrées like his top-notch Maryland crab cakes—loosely
packed jumbo lumps of crab enveloped in a crisp, light crust with peppery Old Bay
style seasoning. Or try his linguine with shrimp, chicken and sun-dried tomatoes in
a lemon garlic oil. Delicious freshly made desserts and espresso round out your meal.
At Berry and Elliott's you'll feel like an honored guest at a sophisticated private home—
a delightful experience.

Windows Restaurant

202 East Pratt Street, Baltimore, Maryland
410-547-1200

BUSINESS SEASON: all year
HOURS: open daily for breakfast, lunch, and dinner
WATERVIEW: Inner Harbor/Patapsco River
CREDIT CARDS: AE, DC, Disc, MC, Visa
HOUSE SPECIALTIES: Chesapeake Bay crab chowder, fried calamari, baked oysters, pan-roasted mussels, raw bar assortment, pan-seared duck breast, seafood Cioppino, Caribbean jerk spice rack of lamb, Maryland crab cakes

History along the Patapsco River began with early Indian camps and continues with the present harbor revitalization. The Patapsco saw the founding of Baltimore, the writing of the "Star-Spangled Banner," the occupation of Baltimore during the Civil War, the great fire of 1904, the terrible flood of 1972, and … the opening of Windows Restaurant in the Renaissance Harborplace Hotel.

At Windows you'll be treated to a stunning view of this historic river and the Inner Harbor in a come-as-you-are atmosphere. Executive Chef Tim Mullen's ever-changing menu includes award-winning Chesapeake Bay crab chowder, baked oysters with deviled lump crab topping, and pan-roasted mussels with pancetta and roasted vegetable salsa. The desserts are also tempting—who could resist Perfect Peach Pie with Sinful Streusel Topping or Chocolate Chocolate Mousse Cake?

11

Phillips Harborplace

301 Light Street, Baltimore, Maryland
410-685-6600

BUSINESS SEASON: all year

HOURS: open daily for lunch and dinner

WATERVIEW: Inner Harbor/Patapsco River

CREDIT CARDS: AE, DC, MC, Visa

HOUSE SPECIALTIES: broiled seafood platter, mixed grill, fried seafood platter, crab imperial and filet mignon, crab cake platter, New York strip steak, stuffed flounder, seafood jambalaya, filet of salmon, broiled seafood trio.

Baltimore is a waterfront treasure with a sparkling harbor, a vast collection of culinary flavors, world-class art museums, limitless shopping, top-notch hotels, invigorating sporting events … and that's just the Harborplace.

When you hit the waterfront, head for the Light Street Pavilion at Light and Pratt Streets. Here you'll find Phillips, whose interior is as delightful as the views from its windows. You'll find antiques, stained glass, and a faithful regular clientele. You'll also enjoy delicious meals made from seafood caught in local waters. The vegetable crab soup is very good and the raw bar oysters are perfect—plum, salty, and ice cold.

I ordered the broiled seafood platter—a delicious medley of shrimp, scallops, fish, lobster and crab imperial. The crab cakes are also some of the best I've found in 40 years of sampling. Try Phillips—the atmosphere, food, and view are wonderful.

Paolo's Restaurant

301 Light Street, Baltimore, Maryland
410-539-7060

BUSINESS SEASON: all year

HOURS: open daily for lunch and dinner

WATERVIEW: Inner Harbor/Patapsco River

CREDIT CARDS: AE, DC, Disc, MC, Visa

HOUSE SPECIALTIES: veal stuffed with Italian sausage, grilled filet of salmon, herb-roasted breast of chicken, shrimp scampi, pizza, pepper-grilled filet mignon salad, Mediterranean chicken salad, warm mixed seafood salad

Paolo's offers a quality dining experience on the lower level of 301 Light Street at the Harborplace. If the weather cooperates, sit outdoors under the green umbrellas and enjoy a view of the foot traffic, the water, the lightship *Chesapeake*, and the National Aquarium. It's also a great spot to watch the water taxi load and unload its passengers.

On my most recent visit, the food was memorable. I ordered angel hair pasta with shrimp and scallops; fresh spinach in a light, buttered tomato and white wine sauce. I followed this delight with a Mediterranean chicken salad: grilled chicken breast with romaine, arugula and radicchio; roasted eggplant, cured olives, capers, feta cheese and cucumber with a fresh oregano dressing. Paolo's is best described as a California-style pasta place, and it offers some of the best Italian food around.

13

City Lights

301 Light Street, Baltimore, Maryland
410-244-8811

BUSINESS SEASON: all year
HOURS: open daily for lunch and dinner
WATERVIEW: Inner Harbor/Patapsco River
CREDIT CARDS: AE, DC, Disc, MC, Visa
HOUSE SPECIALTIES: grilled rainbow trout, Maryland crab cakes, seafood combination
platter, Caesar salad, catfish in lemon pepper, New York strip steak, garlic and herb
fettuccini with clams in white wine sauce, Maryland crab soup, crab claw dip

City Lights Seafood Restaurant is above the Nature Company in Baltimore's
Harborplace. Over the years, Harborplace restaurants have offered a little bit of everything—fine dining, fancy seafood, barbecue, upscale Italian, and so on and City Lights
is part of the variety that makes Harborplace so appealing.

To start your meal at City Lights, there's a wide choice of appetizers including
steamed mussels, steamed shrimp and fried calamari, but my favorite is the crab claw
dip. You may believe that crab claws are just for crackin', but one taste of this dip will
change your mind! For a super seafood entrée, try the seafood combination platter:
crab meat, shrimp, scallops and grilled trout—all succulent and bathed in their own
juices plus a special mixture of herbs and spices. City Lights offers a wonderful view,
delicious food, and a romantic atmosphere. It's a must for all Baltimore visitors.

14

The Chart House

601 East Pratt Street, Baltimore, Maryland
410-539-6616

BUSINESS SEASON: all year
HOURS: open daily for lunch and dinner
WATERVIEW: Inner Harbor/Patapsco River
CREDIT CARDS: AE, DC, MC, Visa
HOUSE SPECIALTIES: Maryland crab soup, New England clam chowder, crab cakes,
petite filet mignon, coldwater lobster, North Atlantic salmon, blackened salmon,
baked sea scallops, strawberry cheesecake, mud pie

The National Aquarium in Baltimore is one of the largest and most sophisticated in the country. Five thousand sea creatures are housed in its seven levels and it's an incredible attraction for young and old as well as a scientific research center.

When you're done marveling at the marine life and ready for some marvelous food, cross the pedestrian bridge and sample the bounty at the Chart House. Indoors, amid nautical artifacts and strong dark wood, or outside with a wonderful garden view, this is a delightful place to eat. The daily fish selection in itself is worth a visit. My favorite is the farm-raised North Atlantic salmon, grilled to perfection and served with aioli sauce. (I had to ask for more rolls to enjoy the last little bite!) The fine food is delivered with extremely smooth service—courses precisely timed and every need anticipated. Don't miss the Chart House.

Victor's Café

801 Lancaster Street, Baltimore, Maryland
410-244-1722

BUSINESS SEASON: all year
HOURS: open daily for lunch and dinner
WATERVIEW: Inner Harbor/Patapsco River
CREDIT CARDS: AE, CB, Disc, DC, MC, Visa
HOUSE SPECIALTIES: scallops Provençale on olive toast, cinnamon shrimp granados,
- steamed clams, mussels Maryland, shrimp pesto, linguine clams, blackened chicken
  penne, tequila barbecue pork and shrimp, pecan crusted lamb chops, crab cakes

Victor's Café, at the Inner Harbor East Marina, is sandwiched between the neighborhoods of Little Italy and Fells Point and affords patrons an incredible panorama of the city's skyline and waters. Owner Victor DiVivo's restaurant-in-the-round has a casual boater ambiance. Dining areas include a romantic candlelit upper level, a lower level and a deck.

Chef Michael Matassa's menu is chock full of unique seafood selections: crackling calamari (flash-fried squid served with the homemade marinara dipping sauce), mussels Maryland (mussels simmered in a red or white sauce with shallots, ham, herbs and spices), raspberry salmon (poached salmon topped with melted brie and served with creamy melba sauce), Victor's Rainbow (fresh baked rainbow trout laced with warm fruit salsa). After dinner, stroll along the docks surrounded by pleasure boats.

16

Lista's

1637 Thames Street, Baltimore, Maryland
410-327-0040

BUSINESS SEASON: all year
HOURS: open daily for lunch and dinner
WATERVIEW: Inner Harbor/Patapsco River
CREDIT CARDS: AE, DC, Disc, MC, Visa
HOUSE SPECIALTIES: Ruben's Garden Chili, Enchanted Quesadillas, Lista's crab cakes,
steak relleno, Santa Fe skewered shrimp, old-fashioned stacked enchiladas, fajitas,
Ribs of Fire, in-the-shell taco salad

In Baltimore's Fells Point neighborhood, restored eighteenth and nineteenth century
residences evoke the spirit of seamen and immigrants long departed. For great food,
no single Baltimore neighborhood offers more choices in restaurants and pubs.

Lista's owners, Kathy and Ruben Evangelista, cook with the freshest New Mexican
chilies, local seafood, and certified "Angus" meats. If you like spicy food, begin with
Ruben's Garden Chili, a low-salt, no-fat blend of fresh vegetables, beans, chilies and
spices served with blue corn chips. Then sizzle with Santa Fe skewered shrimp—jumbo
shrimp dredged in New Mexican chili spices, cooked quickly on a white-hot skillet
and served with rice and charro beans. Crab cake fans will love Lista's—the jumbo
lump cakes are sautéed in olive oil and served with pineapple jalapeño salsa.
Complement your dinner with a Mammoth Margarita.

17

Piccolo's

1629 Thames Street, Baltimore, Maryland
410-522-6600

BUSINESS SEASON: all year

HOURS: open daily for lunch and dinner

WATERVIEW: Inner Harbor/Patapsco River

CREDIT CARDS: AE, DC, Disc, MC, Visa

HOUSE SPECIALTIES: pizza, pastas, roasted pepper bruschetta, Maryland crab soup,
three-tomato salad, lump crab meat casserole, grilled chicken breast, sautéed lump
crab meat crab cakes, grilled beef tournedos, veal scallopini, seafood medley risotto

At the heart of maritime Fells Point is a special place, Brown's Wharf, which captures the authenticity of historic old Baltimore, complete with eighteenth-century-
style architecture, gas lamps, and winding brick walks. Streets paved with Belgian blocks
bear names like Thames, Shakespeare, Fleet, Lancaster and Aliceanna.

At the water's edge at Brown's Wharf is Piccolo's, an Italian eatery with a bright, colorful ambience. On a recent visit I had traditional Maryland crab soup, almost a meal
in itself, served with a generous portion of the most delicious Italian bread and a saucer
of olive oil for dipping. I've also enjoyed Piccolo's three-tomato salad: colorful layers of
red and yellow tomatoes, tomatillos and fresh mozzarella cheese. A few more of the many
choices are available: range veal scallopini topped with fresh mozzarella and fresh salmon
and grilled fresh halibut in a ginger-lemon grass broth with mussels, are but a few.

SS Captain James Restaurant

2127 Boston Street, Baltimore, Maryland
410-327-8600

BUSINESS SEASON: all year
HOURS: open daily for breakfast, lunch, and dinner
WATERVIEW: Inner Harbor/Patapsco River
CREDIT CARDS: AE, DC, Disc, MC, Visa
HOUSE SPECIALTIES: steamed crabs, oysters on the half shell, Maryland crab soup,
French onion soup, scallops tempura, fresh dough pizza, Chesapeake Bay country
crab cakes, broiled red snapper, stuffed filet of flounder, broiled lobster tails

Capture the thrill and excitement of shipboard dining on the SS Captain James
Landing overlooking the Inner Harbor at Fells point. The SS Captain James was built
to look like the container ships that once brought supplies and workmen to Baltimore
from the rest of the world.

The SS Captain James is really two restaurants in one. From Memorial Day to Labor
Day, you're invited to enjoy an outdoor steamed crab feast, steamed shrimp, crab soup
and corn on the cob in the blue-canopied dining area that serves as a landing termi-
nal and crab house. And all year 'round you can board the Captain James 7 days a
week, 24 hours a day and enjoy Chef Mike's specials including broiled entrées, stuffed
oysters, and sea scallops and shrimp Provençale. Don't miss the Captain James … but
if you can't get there for a while, don't worry—the ship's not leaving soon!

19

Bay Café

2809 Boston Street, Baltimore, Maryland
410-522-3377

BUSINESS SEASON: all year
HOURS: open daily for lunch and dinner
WATERVIEW: Patapsco River
CREDIT CARDS: CB, DC, Disc, MC, Visa
HOUSE SPECIALTIES: jumbo lump crab cake platter, imperial crab, steak and cake, soft
    crab platter, fish du jour, filet mignon, shrimp salad, oysters on the half shell,
    steamed clams, shrimp, mussels, fried oysters

Star-shaped Fort McHenry was built in 1776, but it's best known for its role in the
War of 1812. The British had succeeded in humiliating Washington by setting it ablaze
and made their way up the Patapsco to their next objective, Baltimore. In September
1814, they launched an attack on Fort McHenry that was witnessed by a lawyer and
poet named Francis Scott Key. The rest is history. For a commanding view of Fort
McHenry today, pay a visit to Bay Café, on the water in the Canton neighborhood.

Bay Café offers a Caribbean atmosphere complete with palm trees and sand walkways where you can enjoy a raw bar, homemade soups (my favorite is the homemade
chili and seafood chowder), pizza, burgers and overstuffed sandwiches. More winners are
Chef Billy Craven's chicken breast sautéed with fresh vegetables and Cajun swordfish,
both served over rice. If you can't dine in the islands, Bay Café is the next best thing.

20

River Watch

207 Nanticoke Road, Essex, Maryland
410-687-1422

BUSINESS SEASON: all year
HOURS: open daily for lunch and dinner
WATERVIEW: Hopkins Creek/Middle River
CREDIT CARDS: AE, Disc, MC, Visa
HOUSE SPECIALTIES: shrimp primavera, chicken marsala, seafood decceco, broiled
seafood platter, veal parmesan, veal Sanchez, chicken Mount Washington, veal Maria,
broiled stuffed shrimp, crab imperial, seafood Norfolk, crab cakes, steamed crabs

River Watch is a large, very popular place in the Middle River area. There are bars
inside and out and two large dining rooms separated by a huge stone fireplace. The
decor is nautical, with a sailing theme. This is a place where you can sit back, relax,
and watch other patrons pull up in their boats.

Both classic continental dishes and some unusual surprises are featured, and the
Maryland seafood entrées are especially good. The menu includes house creations like
shrimp primavera alongside standard fare such as herb-grilled chicken breast and surf
& turf stir-fry. Another River Watch specialty is Seafood Decceco—shrimp and scallops sautéed with artichokes, fresh vegetables, olive oil and parmesan and served over
penne pasta. It's perfect! There's nothing extraordinary here, just consistently good
cuisine with quality food presentations that will whet any appetite.

Driftwood Inn

203 Nanticoke Road, Essex, Maryland
410-391-3493

BUSINESS SEASON: all year
HOURS: open daily for lunch and dinner
WATERVIEW: Hopkins Creek/Middle River
CREDIT CARDS: AE, DC, MC, Visa
HOUSE SPECIALTIES: stuffed salmon, crab cakes, prime rib, stuffed scampi-style shrimp,
   catch of the day, Cajun buttermilk shrimp and scallops, crab and broccoli alfredo,
   fried jumbo shrimp, crab bisque, veal Neptune, chicken Louisiana

Waterfront dining does not have to mean dress jacket and tie; in fact, I believe fine
food tastes just as good in cutoffs and flipflops! That's why I enjoy the Driftwood Inn,
where the only dress requirement is that you must wear shoes. The Driftwood Inn is
located on picturesque Hopkins Creek, a branch of the Middle River. Owner Jerry
Caldwell has applied his experience as a former builder and construction worker to completely renovate the place and turn his love of food into a popular eatery.

   When you visit, try the Cajun buttermilk shrimp and scallops—they're gently
sautéed with mushrooms, onions, and tomatoes, sauced with spicy buttermilk, and
served over pasta. During the summer the kitchen turns out more than 400 pounds
of king-cut prime rib along with the usual seafood. The Driftwood is priced reason-
ably, and the food is good. By car or boat, it's a nice destination.

22

Decoys Seafood Restaurant

1110 Beech Drive, Essex, Maryland
410-391-5798

BUSINESS SEASON: all year

HOURS: open daily for lunch and dinner

WATERVIEW: Darkhead Creek/Middle River

CREDIT CARDS: AE, Disc, MC, Visa

HOUSE SPECIALTIES: steamed crabs, crab melt, seafood stuffed potato boats, fried hard crab, cream of crab soup, Maryland crab soup, steamed shrimp, steamed mussels, New York strip, fried shrimp, crab cake dinner, steak and steamed shrimp

Owner Tom Cassey opened Decoys and the Quack Quack Bar in what was once Whitey and Dot's, a longtime local landmark. He completely remodeled the building, inside and out, a major project. It's casual and very popular with local residents.

Decoys seafood is simply but consistently prepared in a manner that's worth writing home about. The creamy crab melt is an example: it's a pepper-seasoned crab cake on an English muffin, topped with cheddar cheese and then broiled until the cheese melts. Try it with a cold beer! I've had this creamy delight alone and as part of a fried platter that includes shrimp, flounder, scallops, a small salad and a vegetable. If you're really hungry, try the Belly Buster: a New York strip, a whole Maine lobster, three clams, three mussels, and six shrimp. Still hungry? Top it all off with a classic hot fudge sundae complete with whipped cream and a cherry.

23

Wild Duck Café

Red Rose Farm Road, Essex, Maryland
410-335-2121

BUSINESS SEASON: all year

HOURS: open daily for lunch and dinner

WATERVIEW: Frog Mortar Creek/Middle River

CREDIT CARDS: AE, Disc, MC, Visa

HOUSE SPECIALTIES: Danish baby back ribs, filet mignon, crab cakes, fried shrimp, crab imperial, tuna steak, soft crab dinner, grilled chicken breast, shrimp scampi, imperial chicken, fried oyster dinner, seafood steamer, steamed oysters

A young staff, modern kitchen, innovative American food, a lovely, contemporary dining room and open decks are the dynamics that combine to make the Wild Duck a special dining experience. The minute you walk from the parking lot around to the water side of the Café you'll know you're in a special place.

A raw bar and steamer top off the Wild Duck's menu. Along with steamed shrimp in several sizes are clams, oysters, mussels and a vegetable medley. Other openers include a hearty Maryland crab soup, homemade chili, shrimp salad and imperial sauce, or "skins" (potato skins stuffed with shrimp and cheese or bacon and cheese). The menu includes sandwiches, burgers, more than two dozen dinner entrées, and an impressive "platters" section. I recommend the Chesapeake Special: two filet mignons charbroiled and topped with a mountain of pure white crab meat.

24

Gabler's Shore Restaurant

2200 Perryman Road, Aberdeen, Maryland
410-272-0626

BUSINESS SEASON: mid-April to two weeks after Labor Day

HOURS: open Tuesday through Sunday for lunch and dinner; closed Mondays

WATERVIEW: Bush River

CREDIT CARDS: none

HOUSE SPECIALTIES: crab cakes, steamed shrimp, steamed crabs, fried shrimp, seafood platter, soft crab platter, crab salad, crab soup, new England or Manhattan style clam chowder, chicken in the rough

The deliciously savory steamed blue crabs found in the Chesapeake Bay region are among the most sought-after delicacies for seafood lovers everywhere. One of the best ways to get to know a blue crab (or a dozen!) is to pay a visit to Gabler's. At the end of a winding gravel road, you'll walk along a tree-lined dirt path to a rustic building that will remind you of a summer camp. Although it's nothing more than a long shed resting on cinder blocks, there are few places as picturesque as Gabler's for sampling the local seafood harvest.

Gabler's long tables are covered with brown paper and each table setting includes a wooden mallet and a paring knife … and usually a "reserved" sign, because almost every night the place is packed and the diners overflow onto the spacious lawn, where there are plenty of picnic tables for dining on a pleasant evening.

25

Tidewater Grille

300 Franklin Street, Havre de Grace, Maryland
410-939-3313

BUSINESS SEASON: all year

HOURS: open daily for lunch and dinner

WATERVIEW: Susquehanna River

CREDIT CARDS: AE, MC, Visa

HOUSE SPECIALTIES: fresh flounder orangé, crab stuffed fresh flounder, cold water lobster tail, seafood mixed grill, pasta, veal parmigiana, veal Chesapeake, filet mignon, chop of the day, crab cakes, fresh fish of the day

The Susquehanna ("river of islands"), named after the Susquehannock Indians who long ago lived on its shores, is one of the most beautiful rivers in America. Garrett Island, located under the Thomas J. Hatem Bridge in Havre de Grace, was part of a land grant made by King James I of England. Within a stone's throw of Garrett Island is the Tidewater Grille, where you dine with a view of the beautiful Susquehanna and the distant shoreline.

On a recent visit, the blackboard outside listed Caesar salad, fresh mozzarella salad, smoked Atlantic salmon, crab stuffed potato skins, steamed fresh mussels, and a host of other tantalizing meals, but I chose the Crab Tidewater—lump crab, ham, and sliced tomato on a toasted croissant, topped with Hollandaise sauce. This creamy meal and my seat by the window were delightful.

26

MacGregor's Restaurant

331 Saint John Street, Havre de Grace, Maryland
410-939-3003

BUSINESS SEASON: all year
HOURS: open daily for lunch and dinner
WATERVIEW: Susquehanna River
CREDIT CARDS: AE, DC, Disc, MC, Visa
HOUSE SPECIALTIES: fresh catch of the day, New York strip, crab cakes, crab
    MacGregor, barbecued beef ribs, cream of crab soup, seafood bisque, steamed
    snow crab legs, pan-seared wild rockfish, whole fried baby red snapper

The menu at MacGregor's explains how Havre de Grace was named: The French army officer Lafayette, who played an important part in the American Revolution, was on his way to meet General George Washington. When he saw the Susquehanna and the bay, he was impressed by its resemblance to Le Havre de Grace ("harbor of mercy") in France. He exclaimed "C'est le Havre!" and the name was immediately adopted.

MacGregor's Restaurant is part of the National Historic District. The building opened as the Edgewater Roller Mill in the 1860s and was renovated in 1924 to house the Havre de Grace Banking and Trust Company until 1958. After that the building held many businesses and in 1987 became the home of MacGregor's. Poultry, meats, and fresh fish are imaginatively presented here, the cream of crab soup and angels on horseback are superb, and you'll enjoy it all while you enjoy the view from the large deck.

27

Tome's Landing

600 Rowland Drive, Port Deposit, Maryland
410-378-4005

BUSINESS SEASON: all year

HOURS: open Tuesday through Sunday for lunch and dinner; closed Mondays; Thursday through Sunday during the winter

WATERVIEW: Susquehanna River

CREDIT CARDS: AE, Disc, DC, MC, Visa

HOUSE SPECIALTIES: crab balls, stuffed mushrooms, clams casino, crab bisque, stuffed salmon, crab cakes, stuffed lobster tail, cajun buttermilk shrimp and scallops

The waters of the Susquehanna flow for more than 400 miles, starting in Cooperstown, New York, and eventually fill the Chesapeake Bay. Just before it reaches the Bay, it passes through Port Deposit, so named because it was an active "port of deposit" for lumber and other commodities in the early 1800s. Jacob Tome arrived in Port Deposit in 1833 and singlehandedly developed the town's lumber and banking businesses, which languished after his death in 1898.

In July 1995 Tome's Landing Restaurant and Yacht Club opened atop a well-maintained marina in a beautifully landscaped complex. Tome's Landings' steamed clams with drawn butter are heavenly, and you'll be delighted with the snapper or crab bisque. Try the salmon stuffed with a delicate crab imperial or one of the other delicious entrées. All are served with a house salad, potato, rice or vegetable, and warm bread.

28

Wellwood of Charlestown

Water Street, Charlestown, Maryland
800-621-7995/410-287-6666

BUSINESS SEASON: all year
HOURS: open Friday, Saturday, and Sunday for lunch and dinner
WATERVIEW: Northeast River
CREDIT CARDS: AE, MC, Visa
HOUSE SPECIALTIES: Oysters Rockefeller, Maryland style crab soup, steamed peel and eat
shrimp, stuffed chicken breast, stuffed seafood shells, broiled lobster tails, Wellwood
Seafood Platter, baked crab imperial, crab cakes, scallops Newberg, filet mignon

Wellwood sits in the heart of historic Charlestown on the Northeast River. Across the street from the Charlestown Marina, the white colonial house built in 1843 offers a limited water view, but the viewing inside is fascinating. Turn-of-the-century furniture, lamps, and paintings reminds one of the days of Teddy Roosevelt, who was one of its founders and commodore of the Wellwood Yacht Club. A portrait of the owner, Celia Metz, in a feathered show costume graces the formal dining room. Casual dining is available in the bar, beneath an impressive carved eagle donated by Roosevelt. Managers Christine and Paul Phillips are a wealth of historical knowledge as well as superb restaurateurs. The cuisine is a variety of American seafood and land fare. Ask for the baby lobster tail appetizer, which is not on the menu, but was recommended as a lunch entrée by one of the local diners. The oysters Rockefeller are also fabulous.

3: About the Upper Bay

The Upper Bay on Maryland's Eastern Shore is an enormous, bountiful garden yielding a whole market basket full of products of sea and land, with crabs, corn and cantaloupes characterizing the harvest of the area.

One of the joys of visiting the Upper Bay is walking the streets of Chesapeake City, Rock Hall and Chestertown. Chesapeake City is divided into northern and southern parts by the historic C & D Canal, which opened in 1829 to link Chesapeake Bay with the Delaware River. Today it's one of the busiest waterways in the world.

The Upper Bay's waterside villages exude the charm of the area. Even the names are classic: rivers like Sassafras and Chester flow through towns like Georgetown and Chestertown. The towns of the Upper Bay are within easy driving distance of major East Coast cities, and they're easy to get to by water, too—it's a boater's paradise.

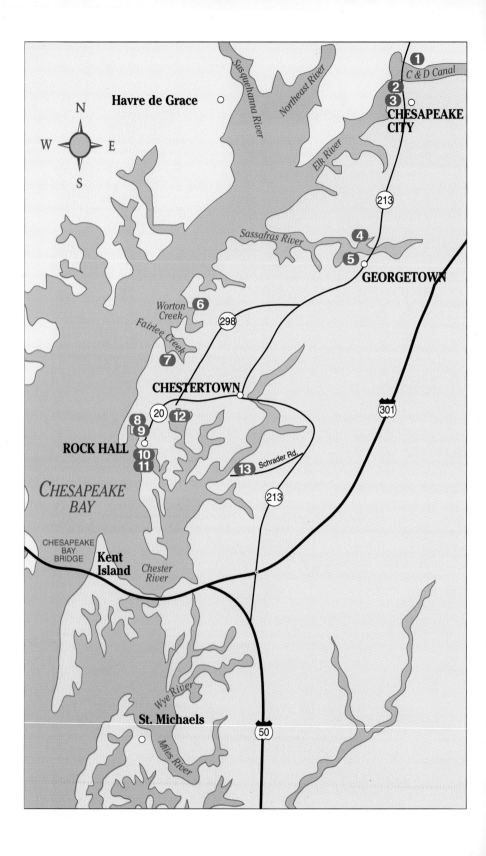

Upper Bay Waterside Dining

INCLUDES: Chesapeake City, Georgetown,
Rock Hall, and Chestertown, Maryland

1. Schaefer's Canal House
2. Bayard House
3. Chesapeake Inn
4. The Granary
5. Kitty Knight House
6. Harbor House Restaurant
7. Great Oak Landing
8. The Inn at Osprey Point
9. Fin, Fur and Feather
10. Paradise Bar and Grill
11. Waterman's Crab House
12. Old Wharf Inn
13. The Sunset Grill at Rolph's Wharf

❶
Schaefer's Canal House

208 Bank Street, Chesapeake City, Maryland
410-885-2200

BUSINESS SEASON: all year
HOURS: open daily for breakfast, lunch, and dinner
WATERVIEW: Chesapeake and Delaware Canal
CREDIT CARDS: AE, MC, Visa
HOUSE SPECIALTIES: broiled tilapia on dill sauce, lobster ravioli on crab dressing,
breast of capon "Florentine," cioppino, crab cakes, sirloin steak with onion rings
and mushrooms, vegetable du jour, strawberry mousse, seafood buffet

The Chesapeake and Delaware Canal links the upper reaches of the Chesapeake Bay
with the Delaware River. On the north shore of the canal is Schaefer's Canal House,
which opened in 1908 as a general store and soon became well known by yachtsmen
up and down the East Coast. The sign over the door read "Joseph Schaefer & Sons:
Everything for the yachtsmen," and indeed it was stocked with everything from food
and drink to anchors and lines. Today, the canal is filled with a variety of pleasure
craft, fishing boats, tugs, and vessels from all parts of the world.

Eating at Schaefer's is a memorable experience, with its combination of nouvelle
and traditional styles. Entrées such as mahi mahi and fresh red snapper stand out,
along with desserts such as peach melba, Viennese apple strudel, and strawberry shortcake with vanilla ice cream and fresh strawberries.

② Bayard House

11 Bohemia Street, South Chesapeake City, Maryland
410-885-5040

BUSINESS SEASON: all year
HOURS: open daily for lunch and dinner
WATERVIEW: Chesapeake and Delaware Canal
CREDIT CARDS: AE, Disc, MC, Visa
HOUSE SPECIALTIES: oysters Chesapeake, Maryland crab soup, quesadilla Chesapeake, Maryland crab cakes, Eastern Shore crab imperial, tournedos Baltimore, baked rockfish, filet mignon, salmon medley

The Bayard House restaurant is the oldest building in this historic city. One of Bayard's mainstays is the Hole-in-the-Wall Lounge, named because a hole was cut in one wall through which drinks were served to be consumed outside. The Bayard House itself is an Eastern Shore favorite thanks to the expertise of Executive Chef Vincent Williams, whose previous titles include Most Notable-Executive Sous Chef at The Homestead in Virginia. The Chef's use of fresh herbs in local seafood dishes has won recognition for the Bayard House menu. (Note that Williams' Maryland crab soup has been a winner in the Crab Soup Cookoff Contest every year he's entered!) His tournedos Baltimore is another winner—twin petit filets broiled medium rare: one topped with a crab cake, the other with a lobster cake, served with two sauces—a madeira cream and a seafood champagne. Marvelous!

Chesapeake Inn

605 Second Street, South Chesapeake City, Maryland
410-885-2040

BUSINESS SEASON: all year
HOURS: open daily for lunch and dinner
WATERVIEW: Chesapeake and Delaware Canal
CREDIT CARDS: AE, Disc, MC, Visa
HOUSE SPECIALTIES: mixed grilled fish, grilled lobster, stuffed flounder, crab cakes,
grilled salmon filet, surf 'n' turf, veal marsala, filet mignon, pasta specialties, lobster
ravioli, seafood salad, fresh strawberry shortcake

Chesapeake Inn's new quarters opened in June, 1996 and it features a conventional menu on the first floor and more casual food, including brick oven pizza, on the deck level. Chef Giuseppe Martuscelli was renowned for his fine cuisine at La Casa Pasta in Newark, Delaware before coming to the Chesapeake. His menu ranges from prosciutto and melon to homemade pasta specialties and grilled salmon filet.

The day I visited the Chesapeake the weather was horrible, but I was greeted warmly by Manager Marco Rizzo, who said, "You look like you could use a bowl of soup." I sampled two—the snapper soup and the chef's blend of vegetables and crab meat, both terrific. Next, my server brought freshly baked bread and a bowl of olive oil for dunking. Then the main dish arrived—the mixed grilled fish: salmon, tuna, mako, and swordfish tossed in a balsamic vinaigrette with a side of homemade linguine. Buon Appetito!

④
The Granary

Foot of George Street, Georgetown, Maryland
410-275-8177

BUSINESS SEASON: all year
HOURS: open daily for lunch and dinner
WATERVIEW: Sassafras River
CREDIT CARDS: AE, MC, Visa
HOUSE SPECIALTIES: oysters Rockefeller, Maryland crab meat salad Dijon, veal piccata,
   flounder Georgetown, crab imperial, soft-shell crabs, lobster tail, Sassafras soup
   sampler

The Granary Restaurant is located off Route 213, just north of the Sassafras River drawbridge. By boat, just enter the scenic Sassafras from the Chesapeake, and it's seven miles to Georgetown harbor along a wide, buoyed channel. Keep watch for the Granary's distinctive cedar roof, and when you tie up at the pier, go in and enjoy a meal with a view in one of three tastefully decorated dining rooms.

Start out with the drunken littleneck clams: fresh Chesapeake clams steamed in a broth of green onions, garlic, ginger, and white wine. Or try the stuffed mushroom imperial—large mushroom caps stuffed with jumbo lump crab meat. The soup sampler includes crab bisque, French onion, and soup of the day. For your entrée, try the Chesapeake Bay trio—sautéed soft-shell crab, baked crab cake, and fried oysters. Desserts include home-made chocolate mousse and The Granary creme brulée with crisp sugar glaze.

⑤

Kitty Knight House
Route 213, Georgetown, Maryland
410-648-5777

BUSINESS SEASON: all year

HOURS: open daily for lunch and dinner

WATERVIEW: Sassafras River

CREDIT CARDS: AE, MC, Visa

HOUSE SPECIALTIES: crab cakes, crab imperial, fish of the day, blackened tuna with shrimp Creole, stuffed shrimp with crab imperial, pan seared chicken, crab bisque, prime rib, poached salmon, pumpkin cognac cheesecake

You can almost feel the ghosts of mariners past in the Kitty Knight House. The original house was built in 1775. Wings have been added and now join the home next door to make lodging rooms, the dining room, and a cozy bar. The ceilings are beamed and the floors are pegged. The current owners believe that Kitty is still present in the home, and in a sense she is—her portrait hangs over a fireplace, resplendent in a lace-trimmed gown. Legend says she refused to leave the house even when the British threatened to burn it in 1813. She met them with head erect and flashing eyes, saying, "I shall not leave. If you burn the house, you burn me with it."

I suggest you pay Kitty a visit and partake of Eastern Shore and Continental cuisine while you watch boats navigate the Georgetown Yacht Basin. The atmosphere is warm and cozy, and I know Kitty's keeping an eye on things.

6

Harbor House Restaurant

43121 Buck Neck Road, Chestertown, Maryland
410-778-0669

BUSINESS SEASON: May 1 through October 31

HOURS: open Wednesday through Monday for dinner only; closed Tuesdays

WATERVIEW: Worton Creek/Chesapeake Bay

CREDIT CARDS: Disc, MC, Visa

HOUSE SPECIALTIES: crab cakes, filet mignon, strip steak, shrimp scampi, fresh fish of the day, grilled tandoori chicken, Portuguese braised duck, beef or chicken curry, roasted pork loin, grilled Chinese pepper shrimp

"Fresh" is the keyword here. Executive Chef Sylvia Sherry's philosophy of freshness stems from her days as a chef/caterer in New York, where she shopped the fresh fruit and vegetable stalls daily. You'll see many repeat customers here, and many diners arrive by boat. Long time local restaurateur Martha Hughes presides over the Harbor House, and her warm, friendly smile makes you feel instantly at home.

To start your meal, try baked marinated artichokes with brie and toasted walnuts or grilled Chinese pepper shrimp. Follow that with Caesar salad—it's one of the best you'll ever try. For entrées, there are crab cakes with sun-dried tomato and lime sauce or a juicy filet mignon tenderloin served with sautéed mushrooms in a red wine sauce. Many items are homemade including the rolls and chocolate walnut pie. Thanks, Martha. Thanks, Sylvia!

Great Oak Landing

22170 Great Oak Landing Road, Chestertown, Maryland
410-778-2100

BUSINESS SEASON: mid-April to end of October

HOURS: open daily for lunch and dinner; Saturday and Sunday for breakfast, lunch and dinner

WATERVIEW: Fairlee Creek/Chesapeake Bay

CREDIT CARDS: AE, DC, Disc, MC, Visa

HOUSE SPECIALTIES: Maryland crab bisque, chicken parmesan, broiled scallops, seafood marinara, New York strip steak, Maryland Eastern Shore crab cakes

Mears Great Oak Landing is a great place to visit. When boaters make their cruising plans, they consider the towns or creeks where they'd like to end up for the evening. Picture the perfect place on the Chesapeake Bay—brisk breezes, sunny skies, and a crew of good friends. After cruising for a couple of hours on the shimmering waters, imagine returning to the perfect home base with an ideal location and all the services you'd expect from a top-notch marina, plus the facilities of a first-class yachting resort. It's not a dream. It's Mears Great Oak Landing, a 70-acre resort conveniently located on beautiful Fairlee Creek. On a gentle hill overlooking the inlet, you'll find the restaurant and enjoy popular meals served in both casual and formal atmospheres.

The Inn at Osprey Point

20786 Rock Hall Avenue, Rock Hall, Maryland
410-639-2762

BUSINESS SEASON: all year
HOURS: open for dinner only. Winter: Friday, through Sunday; summer: Thursday
through Sunday
WATERVIEW: Swan Creek/Chesapeake Bay
CREDIT CARDS: Disc, MC, Visa
HOUSE SPECIALTIES: beef medallions, smoked bluefish, crab cakes, fettuccini with wild
mushrooms, sautéed walnut pond farm raised rockfish, sautéed veal scallopini

The Inn at Osprey Point is on picturesque Swan Creek at the Osprey Point Marina,
surrounded by 30 acres of pristine wetlands. The Restaurant and Inn are patterned
after the Coke-Garrett House in Williamsburg, Virginia, and they're right next door
to the Waterman's Museum, a popular attraction in the Village of Rock Hall.

The Inn's menu changes each weekend. You can expect such appetizers as smoked
bluefish and brie salad with red pepper vinaigrette or grilled jumbo shrimp in sun-dried
tomato marinade on garlic-chive polenta. House special soups include Maryland crab
and vegetable or fresh garden gazpacho. A recent choice was angel hair pasta with shrimp
and basil pesto and a wild mushroom lasagna which was just short of incredible. Another
dinner I'll never forget was sautéed medallions of beef with roasted walnut bleu cheese
sauce and a bottle of Burgess Cellars Cabernet Sauvignon. You'll return soon.

Fin, Fur, and Feather

20895 Bayside Avenue, Rock Hall, Maryland
410-639-2686

BUSINESS SEASON: all year
HOURS: winter: open Friday, Saturday, Sunday; summer: open daily for lunch and dinner
WATERVIEW: Rock Hall Harbor/Chesapeake Bay
CREDIT CARDS: MC, Visa
HOUSE SPECIALTIES: steamed river crabs, New York strip, prime rib, roast beef, broiled rockfish, sea scallops, roast turkey, fried chicken, seafood combo, crab imperial, crab cakes, soft crabs

The "Fin," a family-style restaurant overlooking the Rock Hall Harbor, has open air, screened-in, and enclosed dining rooms, all with excellent views of the waterfront. Specialty seafood is bought from local watermen when available, the kitchen roasts fresh turkey, and the New York strips are cut to order. The famous Land and Sea Buffet offers specially selected seafood dishes each week, and river crabs are steamed fresh and seasoned as hot as you can stand them. Dinners include Eastern Shore favorites like fried chicken and freshly roasted turkey with home-made stuffing, but the emphasis is on seafood—local delicacies such as broiled rockfish and broiled fluke, and premium quality flounders, broiled and seasoned with butter, onions, and green peppers. I recommend the crab imperial, crab cakes, and soft crabs fried in an iron skillet to a light crisp, slightly seasoned. Desserts are good, too—but you probably won't have room!

⑩
Paradise Bar and Grill

5707 Caroline Avenue, Rock Hall, Maryland
410-639-7177

BUSINESS SEASON: closed Monday and Tuesday during winter
HOURS: open daily for lunch and dinner; open Saturday and Sunday for breakfast
WATERVIEW: Rock Hall Harbor/Chesapeake Bay
CREDIT CARDS: MC, Visa
HOUSE SPECIALTIES: old-world brown crab bisque, cheeseburger in Paradise, chicken brochette, fresh grouper, fresh orange roughy, marinated rib eye steak, lobster tail, crab cakes, steamed crabs

"Sumptuous international cuisine inspired by great ports and waterways of the world." That's the theme owners Chris Berghaus and Carlo Fernandes have for their new restaurant overlooking the harbor at the town dock in Rock Hall. Why the bright blue and pink exterior? Chris explains: "We wanted all boats coming in to harbor to recognize the building." Believe me, you can't miss it and you won't want to! The interior has a relaxed Caribbean atmosphere with Jimmy Buffet playing in the dining room and upstairs crab deck. Entrées are international: French/Chesapeake Bay—tournedos de Boeuf Baltimore, Indonesian—cashew peanut chicken, Puerto Rican/Caribbean—mofongo de carne, Australian—orange roughy wallaro, and more. For those who want light fare, there's always a cheeseburger in Paradise that comes with a cool Margarita or a choice of any beverage, domestic beer, or house wine.

11

Watermen's Crab House

Foot of Sharp Street, Rock Hall, Maryland
410-639-2261

BUSINESS SEASON: seasonal: closed January, February, and March
HOURS: open daily for lunch and dinner
WATERVIEW: Rock Hall Harbor/Chesapeake Bay
CREDIT CARDS: MC, Visa
HOUSE SPECIALTIES: fish of the day, baked chicken, prime rib, oyster combo, steamed crabs, barbecued beef ribs, Maryland crab cake dinner, soft-shell crabs, fried oysters, oyster stew, clam chowder, broiled scallops, crab salad

In colonial times, Rock Hall was a stopover point on the road to Philadelphia and New York. Travelers, including Washington, Madison, and Jefferson, crossed the Bay by packet from Annapolis and boarded the stage here. For a closer look at the history of Rock Hall, stop at the Town Museum and Waterman's Museum.

Then drop in at the Waterman's Crab House, where you'll enjoy the acclaimed steamed crabs, seafood specialties, and other delights. The fried oysters, stuffed flounder, and broiled scallops all deserve raves, and salads are a meal in themselves. For example, the Chesapeake combo salad: tender fried oysters and white chicken salad on fresh greens with tomato and egg wedges. Or the crab salad: fresh Maryland crab meat tossed in house dressing and served on lettuce with tomato and egg wedges. After you eat, take the time to walk the waterfront and catch a spectacular sunset.

12

Old Wharf Inn

Foot of Cannon Street, Chestertown, Maryland
410-778-3566

BUSINESS SEASON: all year
HOURS: open daily for lunch and dinner
WATERVIEW: Chester River
CREDIT CARDS: AE, MC, Visa
HOUSE SPECIALTIES: mushroom caps stuffed with crab imperial, creamy crab bisque,
soft-shell crabs, sautéed crab meat with Smithfield ham, steamed seafood
combination, broiled lobster tail, baked stuffed shrimp

The colonial flavor remains strong in Chestertown, considered second only to Annapolis in surviving 18th century Maryland houses. On Water Street, you'll find rows of restored Georgian colonials, and at the end of Cannon Street, you will find the Old Wharf Inn—not 18th century, but certainly with a charm of its own.

The Inn was packed on my latest visit, and though the table was not at the window I still enjoyed the boat traffic and view of the narrow Chester River and the distant shore. While my friend Susie chose from a well-stocked salad bar, I decided on Eastern Shore crab cakes for dinner—large, crusty, no shells, and a pleasant aftertaste. On the drive home, while we were comparing research notes, Susie pulled from her pocket a slice of crusty apple bread retrieved from the salad bar. It was no surprise.

13

The Sunset Grill at Rolph's Wharf

1008 Shrader Road, Chestertown, Maryland
410-778-6375

BUSINESS SEASON: seasonal

HOURS: open Saturday for breakfast, lunch, and dinner; Monday through Friday for
lunch and dinner only

WATERVIEW: Chester River

CREDIT CARDS: AE, Disc, MC, Visa

HOUSE SPECIALTIES: sautéed soft crabs, crab cakes, fish of the day, prime rib, crab
soup, rack of ribs, broiled flounder stuffed with crab meat, shrimp scampi

Rolph's Wharf has been a gathering spot since the early 1800s. Where the marina
is now, was once a steamship station where ships picked up grains and crops from
local farmers and carried them on to Baltimore, Philadelphia, Washington and Norfolk.

Today, people come to Rolph's Wharf to eat at the Sunset Grill. Owners Chef Sandy
and Chip Dreibelbis serve French cuisine in the contemporary style, beginning with
a selection of delicious breads made on the premises. Heavenly creamy crab soup is
carefully prepared from stock to finish and is my personal favorite! Daily specials range
from pan-sautéed soft-shell crabs with Sarcones bread to salmon filets à l'orange. Be
sure to explore the grounds, the old Inn, and the herb garden with its six-foot box-
woods. You may even see Chef Sandy picking fresh green beans or spinach for the
day's meal. It's fun to relive those days of yesteryear, and enjoy the flavor of the Bay.

Quesadilla Chesapeake

3	large shrimp—peeled, deveined, sautéed, sliced in small medallions
3 ozs.	carefully picked lump crab meat
1	eight to ten inch flour tortilla
2	medium shitake mushrooms—sliced and sautéed
2	medium pasilla or Anaheim peppers—diced
½ cup	grated cheddar or Monterey jack cheese
1	onion—diced
1	tomato—diced
½ cup	chopped fresh cilantro
½ cup	sour cream

Mix peppers, tomato, onion and sauté till onions are clear. Add the cilantro and set mixture aside. Combine shrimp, crab, mushrooms and cheese. Place tortilla on baking pan sprayed with a non-stick spray. Put shrimp mixture in tortilla and fold tortilla in half. Bake at 350° for 10 minutes. Remove quesadilla carefully and place on serving plate. Top with pepper/tomato mixture. Dollop a bit of sour cream on top and serve. Serves: Two.

Bayard House.

4: About the Kent Island Area

Kent Island has roots dating to the 1600s, when Captain John Smith called it a "delight-son land," and today's visitor could describe it the same way. Established in 1631 as the first English settlement in Maryland, today it's a destination for seafood lovers, boaters and vacationers. The "Isle of Kent" still harbors shipbuilders, farmers and carpenters—workers who have been so vital to the history of the Eastern Shore.

Tiny Kent Island (only about 20 miles long and 3 miles wide), was once virtually isolated despite the arrival of steamboats and the railroad. It was not until the Chesapeake Bay Bridge was built in 1952 and the bridge-tunnel in 1964 that millions more people began to discover this peninsula.

You'll find plenty of mouthwatering Maryland-style seafood on Kent Island, and this chapter will show you where to get the best ... with a view of the water!

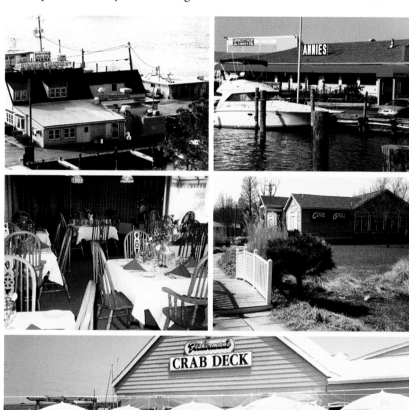

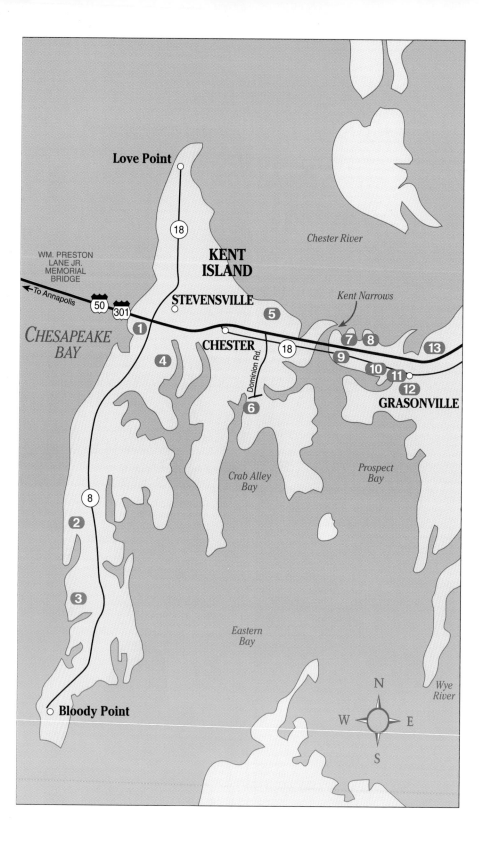

Kent Island Waterside Dining

INCLUDES: Stevensville, Chester, and Grasonville, Maryland

1. Hemingway's Restaurant
2. Pelican Bay Restaurant
3. Kentmorr Restaurant
4. Kent Manor Inn
5. Chester River Inn
6. Wehrs Crab House
7. Harris Crab House
8. Annie's Paramount Steak & Seafood House
9. Angler's Restaurant
10. The Narrows
11. Fisherman's Inn
12. The Jetty
13. Cove Grill

❶
Hemingway's Restaurant

Pier One Road, Stevensville, Maryland
410-643-2722

BUSINESS SEASON: all year
HOURS: open daily for lunch and dinner
WATERVIEW: Chesapeake Bay
CREDIT CARDS: AE, DC, Disc, MC, Visa
HOUSE SPECIALTIES: baked oysters, crab dip, crab cakes, rockfish en papillote, broiled
    flounder, seafood marinara, crab meat tortellini, petit filet and crab cakes,
    Chesapeake mixed sampler, soft-shell crabs

Hemingway's, situated just on the eastern side of the Bay Bridge at Bay Bridge Marina, commands an impressive view of the Chesapeake Bay and the bridge. Sunsets can be spectacular from the breezy deck off the large dining room with its wall of windows. Owner Biana Bellaflores welcomes you to share her love of good food and good times with "Papa Hemingway."

Dinner favorites include crab meat tortellini—homemade pasta filled with crab meat, spinach, low fat ricotta cheese and laced with a fresh tomato and basil sauce. A Chesapeake mixed sampler includes a crab cake, grilled rockfish, clams casino, oyster Hemingway and oyster Rockefeller. Downstairs is a casual grill and bar with a beautiful deck where you can savor steamed crabs, weather permitting. Hemingway's tells a tale of delightful dining by the bay.

Pelican Bay Restaurant

412 Congressional Drive, Stevensville, Maryland
410-643-0230

BUSINESS SEASON: all year
HOURS: open daily for lunch and dinner
WATERVIEW: Price Creek/Chesapeake Bay
CREDIT CARDS: AE, Disc, MC, Visa
HOUSE SPECIALTIES: smoked and grilled tuna, the Pelican Bay Casino, crab cakes,
    soft-shell crabs, fried shrimp, grilled pork chops, grilled teriyaki chicken breasts,
    Maryland crab soup, steamed crabs

It was mid-October when I discovered Pelican Bay Restaurant. I had been here before when it was Bayside Café and again when it was called Jane's Place, but new owners Sean and Tracey Leahy have made many changes. Colorful mums and pumpkins lined the walkway to the front door during my fall visit, and inside the decor was very pleasant, with hanging plants and dark, rich colors. My table was so close to tiny Price Creek that I could almost reach out and touch the workboats, and in the distance I could see the Thomas Point lighthouse.

With my first bite of the Maryland crab soup (tomato and vegetable variety) I knew it was one of the best I'd ever tasted. The chef tops the bowls with additional lump crab and parsley before serving. The location is charming, the food delicious, and the word is out about this place! I know you're going to love it.

(3)

Kentmorr Harbour Restaurant

910 Kentmorr Road, Stevensville, Maryland
410-643-2263

BUSINESS SEASON: last week in February through November

HOURS: open Tuesday through Sunday for lunch and dinner

WATERVIEW: Chesapeake Bay

CREDIT CARDS: AE, Disc, MC, Visa

HOUSE SPECIALTIES: steamed crabs, chargrilled sirloin, prime rib, crab alfredo, penne
with crab and shrimp, soft-shell crabs, crab combo, fresh fish of the day, stuffed fish
of the day

"The menu proclaims happiness is Kentmorr," and happy are those who take time
to discover this popular Eastern Shore eatery. My friend Susie Wills and I visited for
lunch and opened with the hot crab dip—beautiful crab meat in a creamy sauce. The
Old Bay Seasoning and the horseradish, along with a splash of Tabasco, gave it just the
right amount of heat. Susie said, "I'm full already," but she was able to finish a fresh
crab meat salad, tossed in a special dressing and served on a bed of greens and sliced
hard boiled egg. I went for the Luncheon Special—a bowl of Maryland red crab soup
and a fried soft-shell crab sandwich.

Two days later I returned with friends Jose Garnham and Pat Piper, and we opted
for the traditional Maryland steamed hardshell crabs with fiery Baltimore spices. Perfect
again! Do you want to get happy? Get to Kentmorr Restaurant.

4

Kent Manor Inn

500 Kent Manor Drive, Stevensville, Maryland
410-643-5757 • 800-820-4511

BUSINESS SEASON: all year
HOURS: open daily for lunch and dinner
WATERVIEW: Thompson Creek/Eastern Bay
CREDIT CARDS: AE, DC, Disc, MC, Visa
HOUSE SPECIALTIES: Elizabethan scampi, seared breast of duck, hot Maryland crab and
   artichoke heart compote, Maryland crab cakes, braised rabbit hunter-style, seared
   blackened sirloin

The Eastern Shore is quiet, peaceful countryside of flat farmlands, historic towns,
and unspoiled waterside villages. To see what life was like in 1820, spend some time
at Kent Manor Inn, where the simple pleasures of summers past have not vanished.
This grand old mansion was originally created with romance, serenity, and country
elegance, and present owners David Meloy and Alan Michaels maintain the tradition
in their four cozy Victorian dining rooms and an enclosed water-view solarium.

Here's a sample of the dishes prepared by Executive Chef Dennis Shakan. For appetizers, try the Elizabethan scampi—jumbo shrimp brushed with horseradish sauce, bacon-
wrapped, and finished with a vermouth concasse—and don't think of passing up the
cream of crab soup with a side of sherry. For entrées, I suggest the jumbo lump crab
cakes or a caramelized Vidalia onion and Maryland baby corn sauce. Need I say more?

Chester River Inn

205 Tackle Circle, Chester, Maryland
410-643-3886

BUSINESS SEASON: all year

HOURS: open Wednesday through Sunday for lunch and dinner; closed Monday and
Tuesday during winter season

WATERVIEW: Chester River

CREDIT CARDS: AE, DC, Disc, MC, Visa

HOUSE SPECIALTIES: pan-fried rockfish, grilled salmon, sautéed breast of chicken, rack of
lamb, crab cakes, grilled tuna, seared tenderloin of beef, mesquite grilled pork chops

Chester River Inn replaces earlier restaurants on the same site (Chesterfield's,
Yachtsman's Inn, and Castle Marina Inn), and the creative cookery of owner/chef Mark
Henry elevates Chester River to the top. During the last 20 years, Chef Henry has
worked in New Orleans, New York and, most recently, at the Milton Inn near Baltimore.

Here's a sampling from the menu: an appetizer of pan-fried lobster and corn cake,
Julienne vegetables and pommery mustard sauce ... the cream of crab soup with garden asparagus—one of the best I've ever tasted ... the mesquite-grilled pork chops
with bourbon molasses glacé ... the timbale of corn pudding ... the chilled black bean
and summer vegetable salad.

You're in for a treat any time of the year at Chester River Inn. Visit several times
a year and sample the seasonal menu changes.

6

Wehrs Crab House

1819 Little Creek Road, Chester, Maryland
410-643-5778

BUSINESS SEASON: April 1 to November 1

HOURS: open daily for lunch and dinner

WATERVIEW: Eastern and Crab Alley Bays

CREDIT CARDS: none

HOUSE SPECIALTIES: great hot steamed crabs, homemade crab cakes, soft crabs, clams, shrimp, Maryland-style crab soup, oysters on the half shell or by the bushel, other local seafood favorites

Discover Kent Island's best kept secret—the Upper Deck at David Wehrs Crab House. David Wehrs is a purveyor of fine seafood and is one of the top suppliers of fresh, local products. When you visit the Upper Deck, you can watch the watermen arrive and unload the day's catch as you dine on the outdoor deck overlooking scenic Eastern and Crab Alley Bays. I couldn't think of any place I'd rather be—that is, until David Wehrs converted an old crab pickin' room into an *indoor* crab house. Now visitors are assured—rain or shine—that they'll get their fill of David's delicious crabs.

Here's another secret I want to share with you. When I want a bushel or two of crabs for home cooking, this is the place I call. Bring your own beer or wine. David will provide coolers stocked with ice for your convenience.

Harris Crab House

Sewards Point Road, Grasonville, Maryland
410-827-9500

BUSINESS SEASON: all year
HOURS: open daily for lunch and dinner
WATERVIEW: Kent Narrows/Chester River
CREDIT CARDS: MC, Visa
HOUSE SPECIALTIES: backfin crab cakes, crab imperial, steamed crabs, barbecued
  chicken and ribs, crab soup (both cream-based and traditional Maryland style),
  steamed shrimp platter, broiled rockfish

There was a time when boaters traveling from the Chester River to the Eastern Bay considered Kent Narrows a problem rather than a destination. That has changed, thanks largely to a new 65-foot-high bridge that now spans the Narrows. Early diners at Harris Crab House catch the sunset, a spectacular show from the dining room. These are also great seats for watching an endless parade of boats, and, of course, for partaking in the delicious homemade food prepared here.

I can recommend the jumbo backfin crab cakes, the crab imperial, the rich cream of crab soup … and the hot steamed crabs aren't bad either. I enjoy the Harris' special blend of seafood seasoning. Before or after your meal, don't miss the Harris Channel Market right next door. It's attached to the old packing house and is full of quaint and unique shops ideal for browsing and shopping for all sorts of goodies.

⑧

Annie's Paramount Steak & Seafood House

500 Kent Narrows Way North, Grasonville, Maryland
410-827-7103

BUSINESS SEASON: all year
HOURS: open daily for lunch and dinner
WATERVIEW: Kent Narrows/Chester River
CREDIT CARDS: MC, Visa
HOUSE SPECIALTIES: top sirloin, filet mignon, prime rib, New York strip and porterhouse
 steak, veal Fontanela, veal scallopini, cold water lobster tail, filet of haddock, spiced
 shrimp dinner

Annie's, owned by Mike Katinas and family, traces its roots to downtown Washington DC. Annie's is very popular—on a recent visit, the main dining room was full and our group was seated in the back dining room.

Annie's meals begin with salads made fresh daily using the finest produce available. They're a crisp, delicious combination of romaine, leaf, and iceberg lettuces and other garden-fresh vegetables. Entrées include many Angus beef specialties. Annie's prime ribs of beef, dry-aged for three weeks before being cooked in specially designed ovens, are famous for their flavor and tenderness. If you're a seafood lover but don't want to pass up a great steak, I suggest you try the steak and seafood platter—a homemade jumbo lump crab cake plus a char-broiled top sirloin.

Angler's Restaurant

Route 18, Grasonville, Maryland
401-827-6717

BUSINESS SEASON: all year
HOURS: open daily for breakfast, lunch, and dinner
WATERVIEW: Kent Narrows/Prospect Bay
CREDIT CARDS: Disc, MC, Visa
HOUSE SPECIALTIES: soft crab sandwich, seafood platter, crab cakes, fried shrimp, oyster stew, crab soup, clam chowder, fried oysters, scallops, fried clams, daily specials, roast beef, rib eye, fried chicken

Angler's Restaurant and Marina is located on the south side of Kent Narrows Bridge at the end of Route 18. It's a delightful, downhome kind of place that caters to the watermen who work the Chesapeake Bay.

At breakfast, you can expect to find a waterman at every table. If it's wintertime and the winds are blowing hard, you may see them still sitting there at lunchtime—their plates piled high with crispy fried oysters, fried shrimp, or fried clams. The old pine paneling and mahogany woodwork add to the atmosphere by reflecting the lights in a warm, golden glow.

On my last visit, the special of the day was Salisbury steak with mashed potatoes, a vegetable, rolls and butter—and it was under five dollars. Don't expect anything fancy, but do expect good food, good people, and a rustic, watermen's atmosphere.

10

The Narrows

3023 Kent Narrows Way, Grasonville, Maryland
301-827-8113

BUSINESS SEASON: all year
HOURS: open daily for lunch and dinner
WATERVIEW: Kent Narrows/Prospect Bay
CREDIT CARDS: DC, DISC, MC, VISA
HOUSE SPECIALTIES: Crab soup, crab cakes, crab imperial, seafood primavera, filet
   mignon with broiled crab cake, crusted rack of lamb, fried oysters, combos, crab
   cake & ham, crab cake & oysters, crab cake & soft clams

In August, 1631 William Claiborne landed upon the Isle of Kent and contracted
with the natives for their rights to possess the land for the Crown of England. Kent
Island's heritage is very much a part of life on the island.

An Eastern Shore favorite since opening in the fall of 1983, The Narrows is a grace-
ful replacement for the former "Shucking House." On our most recent visit we were led
to window seats where our view of Prospect Bay set the mood for the food to come. The
award-winning crab soup was marvelous, and I like adding my own sherry. Oyster
Rockefeller followed, complemented by a glass of Joseph Phelps Vineyards '91 Johannesburg
Riesling. For a main course, I selected the shrimp salad—jumbo shrimp topped by a tangy
dressing and served on a bed of crisp lettuce. The Narrows offers a fine, experienced kitchen
staff that presents innovative, dishes attractive to the eye as well as the palate.

11

Fisherman's Inn Restaurant

3116 Main Street (Rt. 18), Grasonville, Maryland
410-827-8807 • Crab Deck—410-827-6666

BUSINESS SEASON: all year

HOURS: open daily for lunch and dinner

WATERVIEW: Kent Narrows/Prospect Bay

CREDIT CARDS: AE, Disc, MC, Visa

HOUSE SPECIALTIES: oysters, clams and fish prepared traditionally (stuffed flounder and
   rockfish are favorites); an array of dishes prepared with shrimp, scallops, lobster;
   juicy prime rib (available on weekends), steamed crabs

Back in 1930, when Kent Narrows was nothing more than a marsh full of muskrats,
Captain Alex Thomas and his wife Mae opened the original Fisherman's Inn with seating for 30. They lived upstairs with their two children, often renting their own bed-
rooms to anglers while they slept on the front porch swing. In 1939, they added a
second floor with more guest rooms, and when the Chesapeake Bay Bridge opened
in 1952, a new screened porch created more seats for hungry diners. The Thomas's
daughter and son-in-law built the new, larger restaurant in 1971, and reconstructed
it after a fire destroyed the restaurant on December 23, 1980. In the summer of 1991,
Fisherman's Crab Deck became the latest addition to what has become "Fisherman's
Village." Now an Eastern Shore landmark run by a third generation of the family,
Fisherman's Inn offers delicious food and friendly service.

⑫
The Jetty Restaurant
Wells Cove Road, Grasonville, Maryland
410-827-8225

BUSINESS SEASON: all year
HOURS: open daily for lunch and dinner
WATERVIEW: Kent Narrows/Prospect Bay
CREDIT CARDS: Disc, MC, Visa
HOUSE SPECIALTIES: jumbo crab cakes sandwich, spicy steamed shrimp, crab soup, shrimp salad, seafood chowder, hot & spicy shrimp, cherrystone clams, half-pound fried fish sandwich, steamed crabs

The Jetty, so named because it sits on a point of land surrounded by water on three sides, is a great place to catch a glimpse of the quiet land nestled between the Chester River and Prospect Bay. You'll see some boats napping in the harbor and others heading in and out of the Kent Narrows Channel. Inside I found a long, friendly bar, a couple of pool tables, and a somewhat loud jukebox. The Jetty is as informal as you can get, but I could tell everyone was having fun. I made my way through the small dining area and out to the large deck.

When it's time to eat, try a bowl of steaming crab soup and a jumbo crab cake sandwich. It's a whopping five ounces of lump crab meat, and the management is quick to point out that "our filler is backfin." It comes served on a soft potato roll with lettuce, tomato, fries and cole slaw. I can't wait to go back.

(13)

Cove Grill

411 Winchester Creek Road, Grasonville, Maryland
410-827-7800

BUSINESS SEASON: all year
HOURS: open daily for lunch and dinner
WATERVIEW: Winchester Creek/Chester River
CREDIT CARDS: AE, DC, MC, Visa
HOUSE SPECIALTIES: crab and artichoke dip, crab cakes, broiled flounder, broiled
   scallops, pecan chicken, country style barbecued ribs, combination platters, chicken
   popover, veal Chesapeake, fried seafood platter, filet mignon

The Eastern Shore is considered the land of gracious living, and you can tell this by
the number of outstanding restaurants that dot the shore. One is the Cove Grill, part
of a resort that includes the Queenstown Harbor Golf Links. The entrance is down
a pleasant pine-sheltered walkway, across a wooden foot bridge, and then through a
lovely foyer. There's one large dining room with additional seating on an outdoor deck.

When my waitress informed me that the soup of the day was cream of crab, I couldn't
resist. It was served piping hot, with a large crab claw on top. The soup was loaded
with crab meat and tiny cuts of beef that added gusto. The Cove is also known for
an Eastern Shore favorite—Veal Chesapeake: fresh sautéed veal topped with backfin
crab and crowned with hollandaise sauce.

Hell's Kitchen Crabcakes

1 lb.	jumbo lump crab meat
⅓ cup	fresh parsley, chopped
1	large egg
¼ cup	mayonnaise
1 tsp.	Worcestershire sauce
1 tsp.	Old Bay seasoning
⅓ cup	Italian bread crumbs

Remove shells from crab meat, add chopped parsley and mix. Set aside. (When handling crab meat, try not to break up the lumps.)
Wisk egg, mayonnaise, Worcestershire and Old Bay seasoning together. Add egg and mayonnaise mixture to crab meat a little at a time until moderately moist (not wet). Mix in just enough of the bread crumbs to hold the mixture together. Form crab cakes. Yield: Five crab cakes. Broil or fry, whichever you prefer.

Wehrs Crab House.

5: About the St. Michaels Area

In the early 1800s, St. Michaels was famous for its Baltimore clippers—the sleekest sailing vessels built at the time. Tilghman Island also figures strongly in the area's history. Once thousands of skipjacks worked its waters, but today the number has shrunk to less than 20, comprising the last commercial sailing fleet in the nation. Tiny Oxford was an official port of entry in pre-Revolutionary days, and is still an important center for boatbuilding and yachting as well as a protected harbor for watermen.

In summer, Tilghman Island, Oxford and St. Michaels are host to a cloud of sail as yachtsmen from all over the world drop anchor. St. Michaels, has become much more popular since 1965, when the Chesapeake Bay Maritime Museum was established. Quality seafood is served throughout the area with Colonial charm ... and with a wonderful view of the water.

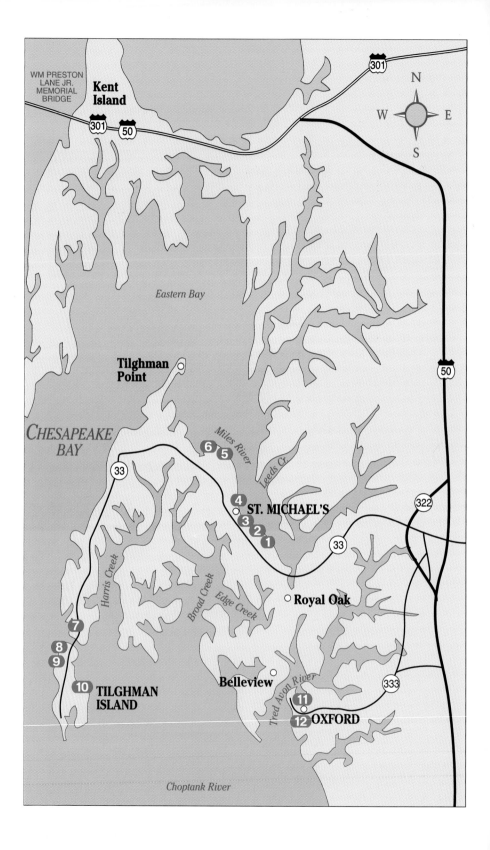

St. Michaels Waterside Dining

INCLUDES: St. Michaels, Tilghman Island, and Oxford, Maryland.

1. Windows
2. Town Dock Restaurant
3. St. Michaels Crab House
4. The Crab Claw Restaurant
5. The Inn at Perry Cabin
6. Bayview—Harbourtowne
7. Bay Hundred Restaurant
8. Osprey Restaurant
9. The Tilghman Island Inn
10. Harrison's Chesapeake House
11. Schooners Llanding
12. Pier Street Restaurant

❶
Windows

101 North Harbor Road, St. Michaels, Maryland
410-745-5102

BUSINESS SEASON: all year

HOURS: open daily for breakfast, lunch, and dinner

WATERVIEW: St. Michaels Harbor/Miles River

CREDIT CARDS: AE, Disc, MC, Visa

HOUSE SPECIALTIES: grilled marinated pork tenderloin, rack of lamb, grilled salmon steak, lighthouse crab cakes, garlic crab dip, sauteed soft-shell crabs, black Angus center cut steak

Ψ ❦ ⚓ ♿ ☎

Windows is part of St. Michaels Harbor Inn and Marina. Next to Chesapeake Bay Maritime Museum's famed "Hooper Straight" Lighthouse, this beautiful glass-enclosed restaurant overlooks the harbor from a second-floor location. Windows offers more than just a lovely location with a great view of the waterfront activity—it offers great food as well.

Why not begin your meal with a chef specialty: cream of crab soup with a sherry base. A Windows salad should follow: red leaf and romaine lettuce, field onions, marinated red onion, carrots, and tomato, or maybe a chilled penne pasta with garden vegetables, feta cheese, all tossed in a tomato herb dressing. As a main course, I suggest the crab and shrimp imperial topped with dijon sabayon—or if you time your visit like I did mine, the sautéed soft-shell crabs in herb lemon butter can't be beat.

②

Town Dock Restaurant

125 Mulberry Street, St. Michaels, Maryland
410-745-5577

BUSINESS SEASON: all year
HOURS: open daily for lunch and dinner
WATERVIEW: St. Michaels Harbor/Miles River
CREDIT CARDS: AE, CB, DC, Disc, MC, Visa
HOUSE SPECIALTIES: rack of lamb, roast duck breast, vegetable stew, catch of the day, crab cakes, crab imperial, soft-shell crabs, Maine lobster, veal of the day, filet mignon, surf 'n' turf, roast chicken

Change occurs slowly on the geographically isolated Eastern Shore, but one fortuitous recent change happened in 1994 when the Town Dock Restaurant was purchased by Michael and Betsy Rork (Michael was executive chef at Baltimore's Harbor Court Hotel where Betsy was the catering director) and this experience shows in their menu. Food at the Town Dock is served on the popular deck and in the air-conditioned dining room, both with a panoramic view of the harbor and the Miles River.

Appetizers at the Town Dock are imaginative: the fisherman's crepe is filled with the Chesapeake's finest seafood and laced with dill; seared sizzling scallops are mingled with roasted garlic and caviar and served in puff pastry. If you fancy bouillabaisse, try it Town Dock-style: in a delicious tomato-saffron broth. Twenty-one entrées are offered and Chef Rork prepares the day's catch differently each day. Enjoy!

St. Michaels Crab House

305 Mulberry Street, St. Michaels, Maryland
410-745-3737

BUSINESS SEASON: all year
HOURS: open daily for lunch and dinner
WATERVIEW: St. Michaels Harbor/Miles River
CREDIT CARDS: Disc, MC, Visa
HOUSE SPECIALTIES: steamed crabs, crab cakes, crab imperial, oyster imperial, seafood gumbo, chicken Maryland, broiled or stuffed flounder, seafood combo, steamed spicy shrimp, crab combination dinner

The building that houses the St. Michaels Crab House dates back to the 1830s, when it served as one of the town's earliest oyster shucking sheds. Inspect the lounge ceiling joists for authenticity! The patio bricks outside were kilned in St. Michaels during the late 1800s, and it's been reported the anchors in the landscape area of the patio moored the ships that sailed the Chesapeake waters centuries ago.

At St. Michaels Crab House, you can pick crabs on a brick patio under large umbrellas stamped with the Molson label, but picking crabs is the hardest work you'll have to do. While Eric and his professional staff will take care of you, you'll take care of the crabs, and the scenery will take care of itself. They're dedicated to excellence and consistency in cuisine and hospitality. You'll be able to sit back, relax and enjoy Eric's wonderful food and the delightful atmosphere he's created.

4

The Crab Claw Restaurant

Mill Street, St. Michaels, Maryland
410-745-2900

BUSINESS SEASON: March 17 through November 13

HOURS: open Tuesday through Sunday for lunch and dinner; closed Mondays except
open for lunch April 14 through Labor Day

WATERVIEW: St. Michaels Harbor/Miles River

CREDIT CARDS: none

HOUSE SPECIALTIES: crab claws, oysters on the half shell, clams casino, oysters casino,
crab soup, clam chowder, seafood platters, crab imperial, crab cakes, steamed crabs

Over 30 years ago, Bill Jones bought an oyster and clam shucking house on Navy
Point with the idea of opening a restaurant. Today it's one of the most popular crab
houses on the Bay, located near the Chesapeake Bay Maritime Museum and the historic Tolchester Beach Bandstand.

No visit to the Museum grounds is possible without a whiff of "Summer's Perfume,"
that is, the aroma of steamed crabs being prepared at the Crab Claw Restaurant. So
when the urge strikes, I look for a table on the deck right at the water's edge or on
the open air porch—perfect places to feast on hot steamed blue crabs, sip on frosty
pitchers of beer, and enjoy the vista of the Miles River. Aside from great food and a
pleasing decor, Mr. Jones has created an ambiance that says, "Come on down to eat
and have a great time." Everybody does.

The Inn at Perry Cabin

308 Watkins Lane, St. Michaels, Maryland
410-745-2200 or 800-722-2949

BUSINESS SEASON: all year

HOURS: open daily for lunch and dinner

WATERVIEW: Miles River

CREDIT CARDS: AE, CB, Choice, DC, Disc MC, Visa

HOUSE SPECIALTIES: crab soup, mahi mahi, marinated salmon, loin of lamb, beef
tenderloin, warm braised lobster, filet of halibut with Swiss chard, scallion crusted
rockfish with baby bok choy

Ψ ♥ ⊤ ⍭ ⚓ ♿ ☎

This secluded country inn, built in 1812, slumbers in a beautiful cove off the
Chesapeake Bay. The atmosphere is relaxing and luxurious, and it is easy to see why
Sir Bernard Ashley, co-founder of the Laura Ashley Company, chose this charming
location for the first of his new Ashley Inns in America.

Here's a sampling of Executive Chef Mark Salter's menu from a recent visit: chilled
snow pea and crab soup with scallions and ginger, shrimp and potato hash cake with
seared scallops and lime caper sauce, and marinated salmon filet with a spicy potato salad.
There was more, but I had to leave room for the day's dessert offerings: phyllo purse filled
with glazed apples and pecans served with a cinnamon creme anglaise; chocolate opera
torte with a blackberry compote and a chocolate mocha sorbet ... I don't eat like this at
every meal, but in the name of research, what else could I do?

Bayview-Harbourtowne

Martingham Drive, St. Michaels, Maryland
410-745-9066

BUSINESS SEASON: all year
HOURS: open daily for breakfast, lunch, and dinner
WATERVIEW: Miles River/Eastern Bay
CREDIT CARDS: AE, DC, DISC, MC, and VISA
HOUSE SPECIALTIES: Maryland vegetable crab soup, "House Special" crab cakes, grilled chicken fettucini, seafood platter, jumbo lump crab cake and petite delmonico steak

At Bayview-Harbourtowne, a glass wall faces the Miles River and gives diners a panoramic view of Eastern Bay. The restaurant is at Harbourtowne Golf Resort and Conference Center, a 153-acre waterfront resort with 111 elegantly appointed guest rooms, a Pete Dye-designed championship golf course, swimming pool, and tennis courts. Dine inside or out—either way, the stunning sunsets are yours to enjoy!

But I come here for the food. The Creative Kitchen, under the direction of restaurant manager Nola Willis, pleases the varied tastes of its discriminating guests. Try the Bayview seafood platter: a "House Special" crab cake, fish of the day, shrimp and scallop scampi, and a sampling of crab imperial. Also appealing is the grilled chicken fettucini: grilled seasoned chicken breast atop a nest of fettucini pasta with a light alfredo sauce. Everyone will enjoy this tasteful dining jewel!

Bay Hundred Restaurant

Route 33 and Knapps Narrows, Tilghman Island, Maryland
410-886-2622

BUSINESS SEASON: all year
HOURS: open daily for lunch and dinner
WATERVIEW: Knapps Narrows
CREDIT CARDS: MC, Visa
HOUSE SPECIALTIES: hot crab dip, crab fritters, oyster chowder, tuna tempura, Maryland crab soup, Cajun coconut shrimp, fresh salmon, clams fettucini, chicken corn cakes, sautéed lump crab meat

When boat owners slip their lines and chart a course for the Eastern Shore of the Chesapeake Bay, they're looking for adventure, for the pleasure of life afloat, and for that special country charm that calls them to linger and explore. And when they settle on a port of call, one of the first things they want to do is eat.

May I suggest sautéed lump crab meat with fresh spinach, prosciutto, and fettucini in a three-peppercorn brandy cream sauce at the Bay Hundred Restaurant. it enjoys an ideal setting, located at the foot of the Knapps Narrows Bridge. Owners Donelda and Jamie Monahan add their special touches to other dinner entrées as well—like oysters Donelda: a delicious blend of oysters, fresh spinach, cashews, scallions, fresh ginger, and oyster sauce quickly stir-fried and served over pasta. All dinners are served with a house salad, fresh vegetable, and a loaf of bread.

⑧

Osprey Restaurant

6136 Tilghman Island Road, Tilghman Island, Maryland
410-886-2330

BUSINESS SEASON: all year
HOURS: open daily for lunch and dinner
WATERVIEW: Knapps Narrows
CREDIT CARDS: AE, MC, Visa
HOUSE SPECIALTIES: steamed crabs, crab cakes, soft-shell crabs, broiled rockfish,
    steamed shrimp, shrimp salad, hot crab dip, grilled tuna, soft clams by the bucket,
    cherrystone clams by the dozen, steamed shrimp

Tilghman Island is 2.7 miles long and about three-fourths of a mile wide. Practically everyone on the tiny island makes a living from the water. As you cross Knapps Narrows, the strip of water between the island and the bayside mainland, you will notice docks lined with the workboats that ply the Bay. And once on the island you'll notice the Osprey Restaurant, just to the right of the bridge.

Owner Myles Goger's cuisine features local rockfish prepared with exceptional care. Soft clams, on the other hand, are simply steamed and arrive at your table hot from the pot with melted butter. When I asked Myles about the secret seasoning for his steamed crabs, he said, "It's my son-in-law's recipe." I selected a seat on the crab deck and immediately put away another dozen. In a word—sensational—but be warned, the crabs are seasonal.

⑨

The Tilghman Island Inn

21384 Coopertown Road, Tilghman Island, Maryland
410-886-2141

BUSINESS SEASON: all year
HOURS: open Wednesday through Monday for lunch and dinner; closed Tuesday.
WATERVIEW: Knapps Narrows
CREDIT CARDS: AE, MC, Visa
HOUSE SPECIALTIES: backfin crab cakes, grilled tuna, pork medallions, soft-shell crabs, sea scallops, beef tenderloin, blackeyed pea cakes, quail stuffed with crab and wild rice, baked oysters, oyster and clam chowder

The drive from my house to Tilghman Island Inn is approximately 90 miles. By boat, it's all of 18 miles. On a recent boating adventure, a rampaging west wind ripped through Knapps Narrows—the entrance to Tilghman Island—and the temperature fell 15 degrees in 15 minutes. Captain Pat Piper and I were relieved to see the Tilghman Island Inn ahead. We tied up the boat and headed for a much needed warming spirit.

A good way to begin a meal is with a nourishing appetizer, and my choice was the blackeyed pea cakes served with a spicy homemade tomato salsa. For a main course, Pat had the broiled backfin crab cakes with fresh spaghetti and cumin corn relish. I selected the soft-shell crab platter—smoked, flash-fried soft crabs with fresh tomato spring onion vinaigrette. Fortunately, by the time we left, the choppy waters of the Chesapeake Bay had calmed and we had a delightful return trip.

10

Harrison's Chesapeake House

Tilghman Island Road, Tilghman Island, Maryland
410-886-2121

BUSINESS SEASON: all year

HOURS: open daily for breakfast, lunch and dinner

WATERVIEW: Choptank River

CREDIT CARDS: MC, Visa

HOUSE SPECIALTIES: sautéed lump crab meat with smoked ham, broiled catch of the
day, crab imperial, fried chicken and crab cakes, soft crabs, crab and shrimp
Norfolk, backfin crab meat au gratin

How pleasant it would be to climb aboard a culinary time machine and journey
back into the 1800s on the Eastern Shore where the Harrison family opened its doors
to summer boarders. As guests arrived by steamboat throughout the summer, we would
find Levin Harrison greeting them from his horse and buggy and inviting them to
join him on his daily fishing and crabbing excursions.

From this modest beginning grew Harrison's Chesapeake House, a sprawling country inn dating from 1856. The three waterfront dining rooms extend traditional Eastern
Shore hospitality, and Harrison's continues to provide fresh fish each day from its own
fishing fleet (the largest privately-owned fleet in the United States). Today, fifth generation family members offer their house specialties: fried chicken and crab cakes (a
60-year-old tradition) served with fresh country vegetables and homemade bread.

11

Schooners Llanding
314 Tilghman Street, Oxford, Maryland
410-226-0160

BUSINESS SEASON: all year

HOURS: open daily for lunch and dinner

WATERVIEW: Town Creek/Tred Avon River

CREDIT CARDS: MC, Visa

HOUSE SPECIALTIES: hot crab and artichoke dip, smoked bluefish, baby back ribs, chicken imperial, soft crab dinner, crab imperial, crab cakes, New York strip steak, hot steamed crabs

Since Schooners Llanding opened, it has been the place for locals and visiting out-of-towners to gather. The crowds come to dine and party in an atmosphere that says "Fun." Whether you come by car or boat, you can't help but see the deck and bar with red and white umbrellas. Once inside, you can dine casually in the tavern or elegantly in the waterfront dining room.

For starters I had the crab and artichoke dip—so heavy on the crab I hardly noticed the artichoke. It's heavenly. Among the entrées was a soft crab dinner with *three* soft crabs sautéed and served with rice and vegetables. I love baby back ribs, and the house offering was so tender the meat fell off of the bone, just the way I like them. Top your meal off with one of the homemade desserts—as spectacular as they look. You'll return soon!

12

Pier Street Restaurant

West Pier Street, Oxford, Maryland
410-226-5171

BUSINESS SEASON: all year
HOURS: open daily for lunch and dinner
WATERVIEW: Tred Avon River
CREDIT CARDS: MC, Visa
HOUSE SPECIALTIES: soft crabs, crab cakes, steamed crabs, flounder stuffed with crab meat, steamed oysters, crab au gratin, crab imperial melt, seafood platter, roasted chicken, shrimp and scallop parmesan

Nestled on the banks of the Tred Avon River, tiny Oxford has lured visitors since its founding in 1683. It's a perfect spot for boaters seeking a peaceful, attractive, and slow-paced destination within easy reach of the major boating centers of mid-Bay. If you don't own a boat, a good way to arrive is via the Bellview-Oxford Ferry.

I always stop at Pier Street when I visit Oxford. I'll sit on the deck, have a cocktail, and try to envision earlier times when the tobacco trade filled the harbor with vessels from England. Today, the boats unload daily catches of crabs, some of which find their way to Pier Street Restaurant. You'll get a sample of them in Pier Street's seafood platter—crab cake, soft crab, fried shrimp, clam strips, scallops, fish filet, imperial crab, and fried oysters. The barbecued shrimp is fine, too—skewered shrimp, grilled with a barbecue sauce, and served with wild rice. Wild? I'm wild about this place!

6: About the Lower Bay

The Lower Bay, from Cambridge, Maryland to Cape Charles, Virginia, includes some of the most interesting ports of call on the Bay. Cambridge once was a trading center where tobacco, seafood and muskrat pelts could be bought. Crisfield, Maryland, the crab capital of the world, hosts spring crab festivals that bring thousands of visitors, and here restaurants vie for the title "Home of the World's Best Crab Cake." As you travel south from Crisfield, you'll enter Virginia, whose portion of this peninsula is about 70 miles long and 15 miles wide. Virginia's Eastern Shore is a quiet place where you'll find solitude in rich natural settings, colorful waterfowl, rustic workboats and scenic islands, including Chincoteague, home of the famous wild ponies.

When it's time to eat, search out one of the waterside restaurants in this chapter to complement your taste of this special part of the Bay.

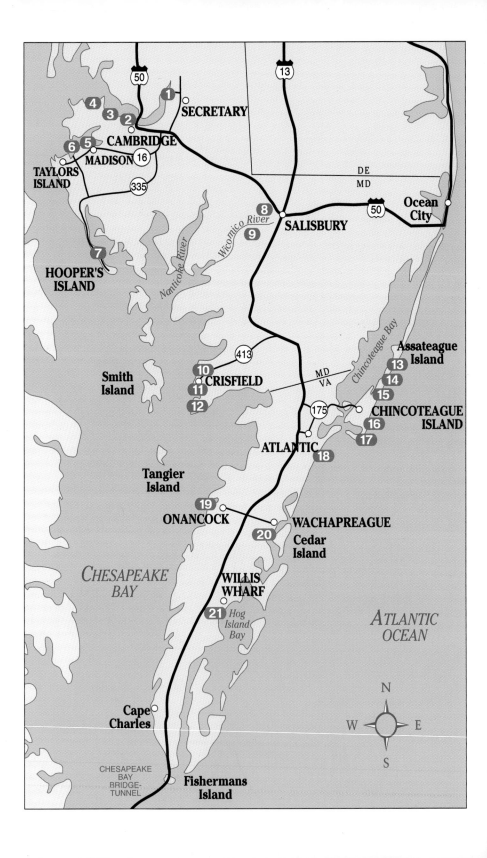

Lower Bay Waterside Dining

INCLUDES: Secretary, Cambridge, Madison, Hoopers Island, and Crisfield, Maryland; Chincoteague Island, Atlantic, Onancock, Wachapreague, and Willis Wharf, Virginia

1. Suicide Bridge Restaurant
2. East Side Restaurant
3. Gale Winds Restaurant
4. Snappers Waterfront Cafe
5. Sea and Sea Restaurant
6. Slaughter Creek Pub
7. Old Salty's Restaurant
8. Market Street Inn
9. Maryland Lady Cruise
10. Captain's Galley
11. Side Street Seafood Market
12. Peppy's Italian and Seafood Restaurant
13. Chincoteague Inn
14. Don's Seafood Restaurant
15. Landmark Crab House
16. AJ's on the Creek
17. Etta's Family Restaurant
18. Wright's Seafood Restaurant
19. Hopkins & Bros.
20. Island House Restaurant
21. E. L. Willis & Co. Restaurant

❶
Suicide Bridge Restaurant

6304 Suicide Bridge Road, Secretary, Maryland
410-943-4689

BUSINESS SEASON: all year

HOURS: open daily for lunch and dinner; closed Mondays

WATERVIEW: Cabin Creek/Warwick River

CREDIT CARDS: MC, Visa

HOUSE SPECIALTIES: steamed crabs, mushroom caps stuffed with crab meat, steamed spicy hot shrimp, crab bisque, crab balls, broiled stuffed flounder, filet mignon, prime rib, crab cakes, soft-shell crab, crab imperial, backfin au gratin

There's an interesting story titled "The Legend of Suicide" printed on the back of the menu here. With a name like Suicide Bridge, you'd expect the bridge to tower over the restaurant, but the restaurant has many levels and towers over the bridge! The upper level is set up as a bar and the new wraparound dining area has two stone fireplaces. There's also a screened side porch where you can sit and pick crabs.

The last time I visited "Suicide," the blackboard at the entrance listed tempting specials: prime rib, fresh rockfish and shrimp gumbo. I was also tempted by the famous crab cakes—freshly picked lump crab meat in handmade 5-ounce patties. But I decided on the crab bisque (I couldn't resist) and wasn't disappointed—it was steaming hot and full of crab. Two things are certain about eating at "Suicide"—you'll find out how it got its name name and you won't leave hungry—the food is excellent.

②

East Side Restaurant

201 Trenton Street, Cambridge, Maryland
410-228-9007

BUSINESS SEASON: all year

HOURS: Open Wednesday to Monday for lunch and dinner; closed Tuesdays

WATERVIEW: Cambridge Creek/Choptank River

CREDIT CARDS: MC, Visa

HOUSE SPECIALTIES: baked crab dip in bread bowl, steamed shrimp, oyster stew, cream
of crab soup, vegetable crab soup, grilled fresh tuna, seafood pasta, seafood
sampler, sautéed scallops

The East Side Restaurant is at the foot of the Cambridge Creek Bridge, near "The
Nathan of Dorchester," a typical and authentic replica of a skipjack that was the result
of a project begun in 1991 by a group of local civic leaders as a way to preserve the
area's maritime history.

Once you've feasted your eyes on the Nathan, feast your taste buds on the goodies prepared at East Side. Sitting on the outside upper deck, wind in my hair and beer
in my hand, my oyster stew was rich and creamy, with plenty of oysters, butter and
chopped parsley. Since one good stew deserves another, I next tried a heaping bowl
of vegetable crab soup. When I found out the cream of crab soup was sold out, I selected
a tray of steamed oysters instead. But guess what? East Side Manager Diane Davie
saw to it that a bowl of cream of crab was on its way.

❸
Gale Winds Restaurant

203 Trenton Street, Cambridge, Maryland
410-221-1086

BUSINESS SEASON: all year
HOURS: open Tuesday through Sunday for lunch and dinner; closed Mondays
WATERVIEW: Cambridge Creek/Choptank River
CREDIT CARDS: MC, Visa
HOUSE SPECIALTIES: crab cakes, crab imperial, single fried oysters, seafood gumbo, broiled scallops, soft-shell crab, surf and turf, charbroiled chicken breast, New York strip, prime rib, look for the daily specials

Owner Gale Olsen told me, "I was an optician for 37 years, but I had my eyes on this place and when it went up for sale; I was ready to make a change. So here I am." When I arrived, it looked like the place was closed. When I walked around the building to watch the boat traffic on Cambridge Creek, I noticed workers inside. When I told them I thought they were closed, I was told, "When the flag's flying out front, we're open." So when in doubt, look for the flag. And when you place your order, look for the soft-shell crabs. This is a special treat. They come served with crispy salad and choice of two vegetables. I requested that they be served on two pieces of plain white bread. They were excellent and came with chips and pickle. So good were they that I could have eaten two more! I selected the cream of crab soup instead. The cole slaw is one of the best I've tasted, and the desserts, especially the apple pie, are very good.

④
Snappers Waterfront Cafe

112 Commerce Street, Cambridge, Maryland
410-228-0112

BUSINESS SEASON: all year

HOURS: open daily for lunch and dinner

WATERVIEW: Cambridge Creek/Choptank River

CREDIT CARDS: AE, MC, Visa

HOUSE SPECIALTIES: crab dip, crab balls, the blooming onion, seafood nachos, steak or chicken fajitas, seafood enchiladas, prime rib, New York strip steak, chicken Chesapeake, jumbo lump crab cakes, crab imperial, seafood Norfolk fettuccini

In 1900, there were 2000 skipjacks on the Bay, and they filled Cambridge Harbor. By 1980 there were only 40; today there are less than 20. The *Lady Katie*, pictured below, is a wooden sailboat designed especially to dredge for oysters in shallow water.

Snappers is a new and trendy addition to the charming Cambridge waterfront that specializes in Maryland seafood and American and Southwestern cuisine. When owner John (Syd) Sydnor wants crab meat, he simply walks next door to J. M. Clayton Co. Seafood, established in 1890—the last crab-processing factory on Cambridge Creek. On a recent visit, I began with a pint of Cambridge's own Wild Goose Porter and couldn't resist the "Blooming Onion," a large onion cut into a flower, batter dipped, fried till golden, and served with a delicious dipping sauce. Then came a cup of vegetable beef crab soup and broiled jumbo cakes of pure seasoned lump crab meat. Delicious!

⑤

Sea and Sea Restaurant

Route 16, Madison, Maryland
410-228-4111

BUSINESS SEASON: all year
HOURS: open daily for lunch and dinner
WATERVIEW: Madison Bay/Little Choptank River
CREDIT CARDS: AE, MC, Visa
HOUSE SPECIALTIES: crab balls, crab cakes, steamed crabs, single fried oysters, fried
   chicken, seafood combo, New York strip, roast beef, flounder, catfish, veal cutlet,
   baked ham

The best way to approach this part of Bay Country is with map in hand, a full tank of gas, and no set agenda. Pick a road and follow it to whatever experience it takes you to. Most people who venture from Route 50 in Cambridge head to the Blackwater National Wildlife Refuge, which gets most of its visitors during the fall and winter. People come to see the area's other visitors—thousands of migratory waterfowl, including Canada and snow geese. In summer, the trip is still worthwhile—on the ground you'll see great blue heron, deer, and Delaware fox squirrel—and in the sky you may be lucky and see an eagle. This is the leading area for nesting bald eagles on the East Coast. Even if you don't see one, keep your eyes open for the Sea and Sea Restaurant, part of the Madison Bay Marina and Campground. It's a casual eatery that specializes in steamed crabs and single fried oysters, plus other delectables from the local waters.

6

Slaughter Creek Pub

Route 16, Taylor's Island, Maryland
410-221-2911

BUSINESS SEASON: all year
HOURS: open daily for breakfast, lunch, and dinner
WATERVIEW: Slaughter Creek/Little Choptank River
CREDIT CARDS: none
HOUSE SPECIALTIES: turkey club sandwich, crab cake sandwich, soft-shell crab
sandwich, chicken cordon bleu, crab balls, fish of the day sandwich, barbecued
chicken, chili, potato soup, homemade chicken noodle soup

Taylor's Island, named by John Taylor in 1662, consists of several islands separated by
Slaughter Creek, which twists southward to the Honga River. History flourishes here,
with local pirates, Dutch shipwrecks, Spanish coins, and battles with the British. At the
lower end of Slaughter Creek lies a small wildlife management area. Located on Route
16 just across the Slaughter Creek Bridge is Taylor's Island Trading Co. General Store.
Stepping inside is like entering a time capsule, circa 1917, the year the building was
built. The shelves are filled with modern conveniences (grocery supplies) alongside
antiques—all for sale. In the back of the general store is the Slaughter Creek Pub. It's
here you'll find fresh, local hand-picked crab meat sandwiches as well as a selection of
"famous ¼ pound sandwiches … or overstuffed subs"—all at reasonable prices. Where
else could you still get a draft beer for under a dollar? Browsing and barter are welcome.

⑦
Old Salty's Restaurant

2650 Hoopers Island Road, Hooper Island, Maryland
410-397-3752

BUSINESS SEASON: all year
HOURS: open Wednesday through Monday for lunch and dinner; closed Tuesdays
WATERVIEW: Honga River/Back Creek/Chesapeake Bay
CREDIT CARDS: none
HOUSE SPECIALTIES: crab cakes, fried clams, fresh flounder, scallops, soft-shell crabs, oyster puffs, prime rib, seafood platter, daily specials, ham steak, veal patty, Delmonico steak, chicken and dumplings

The Chesapeake area has a timeless quality, a feeling that the past is never very far behind. Nowhere is this more evident than at Hooper Island. Hooper is actually comprised of three islands: the upper, middle, and lower. Some properties on the islands were part of the earliest land grants in Dorchester County. The upper island has two small villages, Fishing Creek and Honga, named for the river that bounds the island on the east. The middle island, accessed by the spectacular Narrows Ferry Bridge, is sparsely settled except within the village of Hoopersville. The lower island is no longer inhabited and can only be reached by boat. Old Salty's Restaurant is a part of the past, but it's also part of the present. Owners Wayne and Jo Ann Ashton bought the old school in 1980 and have made the classrooms into pleasant dining rooms. A meal at Old Salty's is worth a trip back to school!

Market Street Inn

130 West Market Street, Salisbury, Maryland
410-742-4145

BUSINESS SEASON: all year
HOURS: open daily for lunch and dinner
WATERVIEW: Wicomico River
CREDIT CARDS: AE, MC, Visa
HOUSE SPECIALTIES: grilled tuna steak, prime rib, crab dip, soft crab sandwich, crab cakes, shrimp salad sandwich, Reuben sandwich, grilled chicken sandwich, and soup and sandwich specials

Salisbury was laid out as a town in 1732. Today, it's the hub of the poultry, farming, and finance industries of the Delmarva Peninsula. Herons, egrets, and bobwhite quail are abundant along the Wicomico, and another place that's "for the birds" is the Ward Museum of Wildfowl Art, a unique display of fine carvings.

Market Street Inn is the only eatery on Salisbury's waterfront, and there's a full house at nearly every meal. Owners Leslie and Mark Reeves' pledge to provide good food and good value has been carried out faithfully through the years. Each table in the restaurant holds a glass filled with pencils, a jar of Grey Poupon, and a pad of menus. Each menu has a check box to be filled in by the customer. It's a simple idea. On one side is a list of sandwiches, etc., and on the other is your selection of salads, soups, breads, and dressings. You get the idea. Now get on down to Market Street Inn!

⑨
Maryland Lady Cruise

313 West Main Street, Salisbury, Maryland
410-543-2466

BUSINESS SEASON: March through December
HOURS: Monday through Saturday, lunch 11:30 to 1:30; dinner 6:30 to 8:30
WATERVIEW: Wicomico River
CREDIT CARDS: MC, Visa
HOUSE SPECIALTIES: baked chicken, lemon chicken, fried chicken, Eastern Shore
chicken and dumplings, sliced turkey with dressing, baked ham, roast beef, beef
burgundy, lasagne, seafood Newburg, baked whitefish filet

The *Maryland Lady* will transport you back in time to the days when paddle wheelers cruised the Wicomico River. It's an exciting experience for the entire family. *The Maryland Lady* is an 85-foot riverboat with a Victorian decor. The dining tables are conveniently arranged so passengers can enjoy the view while enjoying a meal. The lower interior deck is completely enclosed and climate controlled for season-long comfort. The open upper deck has an overhead canopy and weather curtains and offers the perfect atmosphere for sightseeing and true relaxation.

The menu includes salad, entrée, vegetable, potato, bread or rolls, tea or coffee, and a choice of dessert. A full bar is available on all cruises. Boarding is a half hour before the cruise departs, and reservations are a must.

Captain's Galley

1021 West Main Street, Crisfield, Maryland
410-968-1636

BUSINESS SEASON: all year

HOURS: Open Monday through Friday for lunch and dinner; weekends for breakfast, lunch and dinner

WATERVIEW: Tangier Sound

CREDIT CARDS: MC, Visa

HOUSE SPECIALTIES: crab cakes, crab imperial, soft-shell crabs, broiled crab meat and shrimp, shrimp scampi, sea trout, flounder, Eastern Shore oyster fritters

Crisfield is as far south as one can go on Maryland's Eastern Shore. It's a place where the people, the water, and the land intertwine. Workboats laden with bushels of crabs and other Bay delectables plow the Crisfield Harbor. The waterfront is a living museum of the seafood industry and the culture and heritage of families who have fished the Chesapeake Bay for 350 years.

The Captain's Galley Restaurant is located at the end of Main Street, and from any table you can watch the sunset or a vibrant electrical storm. No matter where you sit, be sure to try the crab cake—the one that made the Captain's Galley famous worldwide! It's made with lump crab meat and can be fried or broiled. If you like fresh fish, try a local catch broiled in lemon, butter, wine and seasonings.

⑪

Side Street Seafood Restaurant

10th and Main Street, Crisfield, Maryland

410-968-2442

BUSINESS SEASON: all year

HOURS: open daily for lunch and dinner

WATERVIEW: Little Annemessex River

CREDIT CARDS: none

HOUSE SPECIALTIES: crab cake dinner, steamed crabs, steamed shrimp, fresh steamed
fish, lobster tail, soft-shell clams, breaded oysters, soft crab sandwiches, fried hard
oysters on the half shell, crab salad, breaded or steamed scallops

"Side Street" is one of those places where the extra touches make the difference. Its
small furnishings are plain; the tables are picnic tables with umbrellas stamped "Bud
Light." The setting is above the Seafood Market on an outdoor deck. But despite its
simplicity, Side Street has one of the best views of the water and some of the friend-
liest service in the area. Within minutes after you've been seated, a service tray arrives
with crab knives, wooden mallets, vinegar, extra seasoning, and plenty of hand towels. It's as if they know eating steamed crabs makes a mess! Most times they're right.
The menu isn't extensive, but it covers the bases as far as seafood is concerned. For a
taste of everything there's the Side Street Special, which includes two crabs, two shrimp,
two oysters, two clams, lobster tail, crab leg, fish, and corn. There's also a Delmonico
steak and surf & turf. For dessert, old-fashioned ice cream sundaes get raves.

12

Peppy's Italian and Seafood Restaurant

821 West Main Street, Crisfield, Maryland
410-968-2727

BUSINESS SEASON: all year

HOURS: open daily for lunch and dinner

WATERVIEW: Little Annemessex River

CREDIT CARDS: none

HOUSE SPECIALTIES: pizza, overstuffed sandwiches, strombolis, crab cakes, shrimp salad, seafood sampler, veal parmesan with spaghetti, baked lasagna, stuffed cheese pasta shells, steamed crabs

And the winner is my brother, Crisfield Bill. Bill Schmidt is a Crisfield resident and has been since 1989. Bill supports local fund raisers, and you don't have to ask him twice to buy a raffle ticket. And sometimes he even wins! I timed a recent visit with his latest victory. This time the prize was gift certificates for dinner at every restaurant in town. Our visit to Peppy's was the weekend of the National Hard Crab Derby, so the town was bustling with visitors. Peppy's is unique because it's the tallest structure in town next to the water tower. At street level is a dining room for relaxed eating, but I like the Penthouse, or Peppy's Pub, as it's called, where there's a great view of downtown Crisfield and the busy harbor, with a 360-degree look in all directions. A part of Bro' Bill's winnings included five pounds of shrimp steamed to perfection, three pitchers of beer, and six ears of corn. We had a great time!

13

Chincoteague Inn

6262 Marlin Street, Chincoteague Island, Virginia
757-336-6110

BUSINESS SEASON: Memorial Day to October 15

HOURS: open daily for lunch and dinner

WATERVIEW: Chincoteague Bay

CREDIT CARDS: DC, Disc, MC, Visa

HOUSE SPECIALTIES: fried crab balls, cream of crab soup, filet of flounder, fettuccini Alfredo, broiled or fried soft-shell crabs, crab imperial, seafood feast, prime rib au jus, chicken parmesan, spicy steamed shrimp, fresh tuna, swordfish, salmon

Scenic Chincoteague Island, Virginia, near the southern end of the Delmarva Peninsula, is where nature lovers find a rare and vast assortment of animal life including shorebirds and the famous Chincoteague wild ponies. A special time to visit is during the annual pony swim, when the ponies that roam free on the island are rounded up, herded across the Assateague Channel, and auctioned off. Across the street and about one city block from the auction block is P. T. Pelican's Intercoastal Deck Bar—The Chincoteague Inn, an island favorite since 1960.

When you visit, try the "trio of shrimp": baked shrimp scampi with golden fried shrimp, and shrimp on a skewer, served with rice pilaf. Or try the seafood sampler: crab meat and shrimp salads served with a filet of grilled flounder. My dinner companion Susie said her soft crab sandwich was too big, but I noticed it was all gone. How interesting!

14

Don's Seafood Restaurant

4113 Main Street, Chincoteague Island, Virginia
757-336-5715

BUSINESS SEASON: all year
HOURS: open daily for breakfast, lunch, and dinner
WATERVIEW: Chincoteague Channel
CREDIT CARDS: DC, Disc, MC, Visa
HOUSE SPECIALTIES: hot steamed crabs, broiled crab cakes, fish and chips, clams and oysters on the half shell, steamed shrimp, crab imperial, seafood platter, stuffed shrimp, crab soup, clam chowder, oyster stew, lobster tail with drawn butter

Thomas Clark has made himself a Chincoteague Island institution with down-home cookin' that's so good he had to open a second restaurant to handle the demand. Tommy packs 'em in for a taste of his broiled crab cakes with crackers and his very own fish and chips. For the food connoisseur, Don's offers the freshest seafood prepared with a small town flair, turning the ordinary into the unique. For example, the Chincoteague oysters are the top of the line. Follow them with steamed clams and spicy steamed shrimp. When available, stone crab claws are flown in fresh from Florida. Soups, served piping hot, are all excellent. Homemade cream-style crab soup and both New England and Manhattan clam chowders are featured, but my favorite is the made-to-order oyster stew. You might also try the Seafood Dream—crab, shrimp and scallops topped with a special cheese sauce and broiled to your delight. It's dreamy!

15

Landmark Crab House

6162 Main Street, Chincoteague Island, Virginia
757-336-5552

BUSINESS SEASON: from one week before Easter to the end of October.

HOURS: open Monday through Saturday for dinner only; Sunday for lunch and dinner

WATERVIEW: Chincoteague Channel

CREDIT CARDS: MC, Visa

HOUSE SPECIALTIES: steamed crabs, prime rib au jus, handcut New York strip, soft crabs, crab meat/Smithfield, whole baked stuffed flounder, oyster platter, crab cakes, Landmark seafood dinner, baked shrimp

One of the most popular sights in beautiful Chincoteague is the Landmark Plaza in the historic pier—today a bustling center of activity that includes a host of gift shops, a bakery, and several restaurants. But the real action is at the Landmark Crab House, a casual place that features some of the best tastes of the Island with a touch of antiques, potted plants, and warm stained glass lighting. The best bites are the Chincoteague oysters—covered with seasoned crumbs, parmesan cheese, and topped with garlic butter. My favorite is the bucket of oyster steamers. For dinner I suggest the Landmark Seafood Dinner—a cup of chowder, golden fried shrimp, fresh filet of fish, crab cake, oysters, deep sea scallops, a trip to the salad bar, and potato of choice. For meat lovers, there's a New York strip hand cut and charbroiled to your liking with a generous pile of mushrooms on the side. Talk about island splendor!

16

AJ's On the Creek

6585 Maddox Boulevard, Chincoteague Island, Virginia
757-336-5888

BUSINESS SEASON: all year
HOURS: open Monday through Saturday for lunch and dinner; Sundays for dinner only
WATERVIEW: Eel Creek/Oyster Bay
CREDIT CARDS: AE, DC, Disc, MC, Visa
HOUSE SPECIALTIES: clams and oysters on the half shell, oysters Rockefeller, clams
casino, steamed oysters, steamed shrimp, fish of the day, seafood-smothered flounder,
pasta dishes, fried Chincoteague oysters, crab imperial, crab cakes, veal dishes

Chincoteague Island is world famous for its oyster beds and clam shoals. This picturesque island is the gateway to the National Seashore and Chincoteague Wildlife
Refuge, and adventure is around every corner as history and legend blend with the
wild loveliness of the seashore. If you're visiting here for the first time, let me acquaint
you with the area. Chincoteague Island is seven miles long and one and one-half miles
wide. Protecting it from the Atlantic Ocean is a chain of barrier islands comprising
Assateague Island, which boasts more than 37 miles of the widest and most beautiful beaches on the East Coast. Assateague Island is well known as a birdwatcher's paradise; more than 260 species of birds are found here. Maddox Boulevard links the
islands, and it's here you'll find AJ's on the Creek. You can expect traditional
Chincoteague seafood along with great taste and service.

17

Etta's Family Restaurant

East Side Drive, Chincoteague Island, Virginia
757-336-5644

BUSINESS SEASON: April through October

HOURS: Wednesday through Monday for breakfast, lunch, and dinner; closed Tuesdays

WATERVIEW: Assateague Channel

CREDIT CARDS: Disc, MC, Visa

HOUSE SPECIALTIES: fresh flounder, local single fried oysters, local scallops, fried soft-shell crabs, crab cakes, crab imperial, steamed shrimp, broiled stuffed shrimp, prime rib au jus

In addition to the unparalleled beauty of tranquil beaches with spectacular sunrises and sunsets, Chincoteague offers fantastic woodlands and marshes. Other island treasures include the Oyster and Maritime Museum and the refuge waterfowl museum. Antique waterfowl carvings and wildlife art are found in almost every back yard, and if you fish, you can choose channel, surf, or deep sea fishing—or go crabbing or clamming.

If you want the freshest seafood prepared by a chef who can turn the ordinary into the unique, Etta's is an island treasure of another kind. It's on the east side of the island—what locals call the calm side. The combination seafood platter is likely to be one of the best you've ever had. It comes with fresh flounder, two shrimp, four oysters, clam strips, four scallops, and one crab cake. Etta's Family says, "Everything is cooked to order. So please be patient when we have a full house." And that's most of the time!

Wright's Seafood Restaurant

Atlantic Road, Atlantic, Virginia
757-824-4012

BUSINESS SEASON: March through December

HOURS: open for dinner only

WATERVIEW: Watts Bay

CREDIT CARDS: AE, Disc, MC, Visa

HOUSE SPECIALTIES: steamed crabs, steamed seafood platter, baked stuffed catfish, flounder au gratin, baked stuffed soft crab, crab imperial, crab au gratin, crab cakes, Wright's combination platter

This family-style restaurant began in 1971 on a site that once housed a poultry processing plant and later, after World War II, a button factory. Although not visible, part of the original structure remains as part of the restaurant. Wright's started out small—with seating for only six people—as a service to the employees of the seafood business next door. Soon other people started patronizing the tiny business and Wright's gradually grew, room by room. Today there are three waterfront dining rooms as well as a lovely lounge.

Wright's is a great place for a special evening with a wonderful view. As you enjoy fresh seafood and bask in the glow of the candlelight, you may see local watermen at work in Watts Bay, the beacon from the Assateague lighthouse, the rising moon, lovely Chincoteague Island, or even a rocket launching from Wallops Island! Enjoy!

Hopkins & Bros.

2 Market Street, Onancock, Virginia
757-787-4478

BUSINESS SEASON: seasonally; closed Sunday, Monday, Tuesday during winter

HOURS: open Tuesday through Saturday for lunch and dinner; Sunday for breakfast, lunch, and dinner

WATERVIEW: Onancock Creek/Chesapeake Bay

CREDIT CARDS: Disc, MC, Visa

HOUSE SPECIALTIES: cream of crab soup, crab cakes, fried oysters, steamed shrimp, catch of the day, steak of the day, lemon pepper chicken over pasta, clam fritters

Hopkins & Bros. maintains a great deal of its early charm. Most of the fixtures, equipment, and showcases are original, and you can even see the office window where, over 100 years ago, you could purchase a steamboat ticket to other points of interest around the Bay. The building still stands overlooking the Creek, and today it houses a museum, gift shop, and restaurant. The walls, ceilings, and floor if the restaurant space reflect the the age of the building. The walls are decorated with old farm tools, tables are covered with purple table cloths, and the floors are purple, too. Outside on the deck area was seating for about 30, weather permitting. My homemade cream of crab soup was pure delight. A Greek salad was crisp and just the right amount. When my crab cake arrived, I said, "What the …!" Hey, it was as flat as a pancake, but boy, was it good! You'll enjoy Onancock, you'll enjoy Hopkins & Bros … and you'll be back.

20

Island House Restaurant

Atlantic Avenue, Wachapreague, Virginia
757-787-4242

BUSINESS SEASON: all year
HOURS: summer: open daily for lunch and dinner; winter: closed Sunday through Tuesday
WATERVIEW: Wachapreague Channel
CREDIT CARDS: Disc, MC, Visa
HOUSE SPECIALTIES: oysters and clams on the half shell, crab meat cocktail, Cap'n
  Zed's clam chowder, Caribbean chicken, grilled albacore tuna, fresh fried shrimp,
  crab cake platter, clam fritters, soft crab, fresh fish of the day, stuffed shrimp

The Island House was a hotel and restaurant on Cedar Island during the early 1900's. It offered sailing, fishing, shooting, and bowling, and with rates of $10.50 to $14.00, it was advertised as a common sense resort for common sense people. The hotel was washed away during the storm of 1933, and the Lewis family built the Island House Restaurant on the site in 1978 and operated it until a tragic fire occurred in August of 1992. Today's Island House, modeled after the old Parramore Island Lifesaving Station, was raised from that foundation and opened in May of 1996. Today Wachapreague is the "flounder fishing capital of the world" and on any given day hundreds of boats search here for this tasty fish. If you want a taste of flounder (or tuna, mahi mahi, sword fish, or trout), I suggest you stop at the Island House. It can be ordered fried, broiled, grilled, or cajun-blackened, and it's always fresh, always good.

㉑
E. L. Willis & Co. Restaurant
4456 Willis Wharf Road, Willis Wharf, Virginia
757-442-4225

BUSINESS SEASON: all year

HOURS: open Monday through Thursday for lunch only; Friday and Saturday for dinner only

WATERVIEW: Hog Island Bay

CREDIT CARDS: none

HOUSE SPECIALTIES: Bayside seafood combo, seafood triple delight, crab cakes, butterfly jumbo shrimp, scallops, prime rib, Virginia baked ham, clam fritters

Back in the 1800s, the tiny town of Willis Wharf was known as Downings Wharf. The name was changed when Edward Willis settled here and opened the E. L. Willis Store. Many of the homes in the village were moved here from Hog Island, one of the Barrier Islands evacuated around 1930. Today E. L. Willis & Co. is owned by Pam Widgeon, who operates it as a restaurant. Easy informality is not only encouraged by Pam; she wouldn't have it any other way. Willis & Co. cooks seafood fresh and unencumbered by fancy sauces or culinary tricks. There are hearty clam fritters and seaside steamed clams—one dozen fresh and tasty. In addition to crab cakes and pan-fried scallops, there's Virginia baked ham and chicken salad. For those interested in nostalgia, the shelving that once was filled with general store merchandise is now filled with an extensive oyster can collection. You're going to enjoy your visit here!

Lower Bay Clam Chowder

24	clams
¼ cup	chopped bacon
¼ cup	chopped onion
2 cups	clam liquor and water
1 cup	diced potatoes
½ tsp.	salt
	dash of pepper
2 cups	milk
	parsley

Drain clams and save liquor. Chop. Fry bacon until lightly brown. Add onion and cook until tender. Add liquor and water, potatoes, seasonings, and clams. Cook about 15 minutes or until potatoes are tender. Add milk; heat. Garnish with chopped parsley sprinkled over the top. Serves: Six.

"That Old Clam Chowder"

That old clam chowder down
on Wachapreague,
is much better
than on Chincoteague.
Eat it once or twice and
love it all your life.
That old clam chowder down
on Wachapreague.

Gilda Hinman
Parksley, VA

7: About the Tidewater Area

Norfolk's harbor, area rivers, and the Chesapeake Bay brought British colonists to this region, whose history dates back further than any other covered in this book, and today the historic waterways enchant natives and visitors alike. A good way to enjoy the Tidewater is to take a 20-minute harbor tour on the Norfolk-Portsmouth ferry.

There's a nautical excitement in the Tidewater area. Stretched along the southern shore of the Chesapeake Bay, Norfolk, Portsmouth and Suffolk are famous for their fresh seafood, including backfin crab, scallops, oysters and flounder. All of the restaurants in this chapter offer a sampling of this bountiful harvest.

All you have to do is select a restaurant, and the rest will happen. You will enjoy outstanding cuisine prepared by master chefs who take pride in the preparation of regional food—and you'll have a great view of the water.

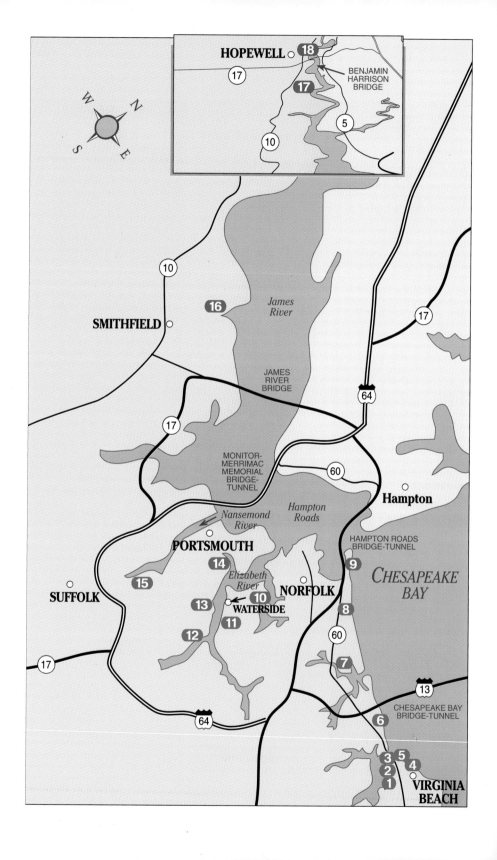

Tidewater Waterside Dining

INCLUDES: Virginia Beach, Norfolk, Portsmouth, Suffolk, Smithfield, and Hopewell, Virginia

1. Chick's Oyster Bar
2. Bubba's Crab House and Seafood Restaurant
3. Henry's
4. Lynnhaven Fish House
5. Duck-In
6. Alexandria's on the Bay
7. Blue Crab
8. The Ship's Cabin
9. Fisherman's Wharf
10. O'Sullivan's Wharf
11. Phillips Waterside
12. The Max
13. Amory's Wharf
14. Scale O'De Whale
15. Creekside Restaurant
16. Smithfield Station
17. Dockside
18. Captain's Cove

❶
Chick's Oyster Bar

2143 Vista Circle, Virginia Beach, Virginia
757-481-5757

BUSINESS SEASON:: all year
HOURS: open daily for lunch and dinner
WATERVIEW: Lynnhaven River
CREDIT CARDS: AE, DC, Disc, MC, Visa
HOUSE SPECIALTIES: fresh fish, Chesapeake surf & turf, fire grilled chicken, Baltimore crab feast, fried oysters, Chick's oyster stew, Chick's steamer pots, deviled crabs, steamed crabs, crab soup Annapolis, chilled seafood sampler

Although it's crowded, dining at Chick's Oyster Bar is fun from the moment you enter its spacious, popular back porch. Out there at sunset, sipping a rum-soaked drink, you can choose from such appetizers as Eastern Shore clams and Gulf oysters—order a half dozen, a baker's dozen, or a bucket. Follow this with the house version of the Baltimore Crab Feast: You start with a pitcher of draft beer and two bowls of crab soup or clam chowder, follow that with a half dozen fiery steamed hard-shell crabs, then two crab cake sandwiches with cole slaw and potato chips. The Feast is completed with two slices of key lime pie. It's a beautiful thing!

Chick's kabobs are two beautiful skewers of fresh shrimp, scallops, and filet mignon served over seasoned rice, finished off with bread pudding soaked in whisky sauce. You're gonna love Chick's.

②

Bubba's Crab House and Seafood Restaurant

3323 Shore Drive, Virginia Beach, Virginia
757-481-3513 or 757-481-0907

BUSINESS SEASON: all year
HOURS: open daily for lunch and dinner
WATERVIEW: Lynnhaven River
CREDIT CARDS: AE, MC, Visa
HOUSE SPECIALTIES: soft-shell crab dinner, crab imperial, seafood platter, baked
    scallops, fresh catch, steamed crabs, lobster tail, shellfish combo, steamed shrimp,
    oysters steamed or on the half shell, chicken limone, deviled clams

Bubba's Crab House and Seafood Restaurant is an institution on Shore Drive and
a tradition in Virginia Beach. It was one of the first seafood places along the beach,
and it's weathered many Atlantic storms and been witness to constant change. But
there has been Bubba's as long as anyone can remember, and Bubba's is known for
preparing the freshest seafoods to your liking. Fish and the crabs are delivered daily
across the Marina docks, having spent the previous night in the bay or ocean. You
can relax and enjoy the best seafood the adjacent waters have to offer inside the rustic dining area or on the covered dock where the sounds of the water birds and watermen will attract your attention.

Once you experience the simple dining pleasures at Bubba's Marina, you'll be
hooked—and your hosts will reel you in again and again.

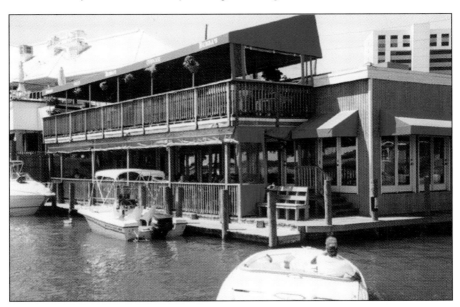

Henry's

3319 Shore Drive, Virginia Beach, Virginia
757-481-7300

BUSINESS SEASON: seasonal

HOURS: open daily for lunch and dinner

WATERVIEW: Lynnhaven River

CREDIT CARDS: AE, DC, MC, Visa

HOUSE SPECIALTIES: jumbo lump crab cakes, she-crab soup, fried squid, clams oregano, oysters Rockefeller, fresh shucked seaside oysters or clams, fresh fish, create-your-own seafood platter, pasta, beef

Henry's opened for business the year I was born—1938. It took me nearly 25 years to discover Henry's, but it's now a must-stop for me anytime I visit the Tidewater area. Built in 1938 on the site of the original Henry's Seafood Restaurant, the present Henry's is a large and impressive two-story structure with indoor and open decks and marvelous views of the Lynnhaven River at sunset. With fresh seafood no further away than the nearby charter boats, it's not surprising that Henry's excels in its seafood. The fresh fish board includes flounder filet, pond-raised catfish, Alaskan salmon, mahi mahi, yellow fin tuna, and swordfish. You can also create your own broiled or fried seafood platter, selecting jumbo shrimp, fresh oysters, sea scallops, clam strips, squid, "old fashioned" crab cake, and a filet of flounder. It's a smart idea I wish more restaurants would try. Henry's has an extensive menu, and it's all impeccably prepared.

④

Lynnhaven Fish House

2350 Starfish, Virginia Beach, Virginia
757-481-0003

BUSINESS SEASON: all year
HOURS: open daily for lunch and dinner
WATERVIEW: Chesapeake Bay
CREDIT CARDS: AE, DC, MC, Visa
HOUSE SPECIALTIES: fresh fish of the day, oysters Rockefeller, she-crab soup, whole
   Maine lobster, roast half chicken, choice filet mignon, Maryland crab cakes, crab
   meat Norfolk, shrimp imperial

"Fresh" is the password here. Chef Joseph Zaremski has been with the Lynnhaven
Fish House since 1986, and he's pleased to broil, grill, steam, fry, or poach your selec-
tions.On my last visit his offerings soanned the globe: flounder (New England), orange
roughy (NZ), salmon (Maine-Atlantic), mahi mahi (FL), yellow fin tuna, (NC), rainbow trout (farm-raised), bluefish (local), red snapper filet (FL), and catfish (farm-raised).
Chef Joseph also creates special toppings and stuffings you won't want to miss: crab
meat imperial stuffing; hollandaise sauce and fresh broccoli; cajun (a unique blend of
52 spices); christo sauce (a delicious combination of fresh tomatoes, artichoke hearts,
fresh mushrooms, capers, garlic, and spices in white wine); Mediterranean sauce (chopped
scallions, parsley blended with olive oil, lemon, parmesan cheese, a touch of spices and
white wine); and more! You are certain to get a most satisfying meal here.

Duck-In

3324 Shore Drive, Virginia Beach, Virginia
757-481-0201

BUSINESS SEASON: all year

HOURS: open Monday through Saturday for lunch and dinner; open Sunday for breakfast, lunch, and dinner

WATERVIEW: Chesapeake Bay

CREDIT CARDS: AE, DC, MC, Visa

HOUSE SPECIALTIES: fisherman's chowder, clam chowder, salty oysters and top neck clams, fried oyster sandwich, crab cakes, steamed whole crayfish, steamed fish

Duck-In has a problem most restaurants wish they had—it keeps gaining land! Until the Army Corps of Engineers decided to straighten out the Lynnhaven's old channel by dredging it, Duck-In's beach was narrow and eroding. The large boat channel was actually between the main building and the gazebo. Thanks to the Corps' desire to keep everything in straight lines and at right angles (and the fact that Duck-In's deed goes to the low water line), they have gained nearly three acres of land since the late fifties.

This restaurant attracts more than 300,000 customers each year and was the people's choice for 25 "Best of the Beach" awards in only 4 years. It's up to you to pay a visit and prepare for an American dining experience that has won raves from nearly every publication and reviewer in the state.

6

Alexander's on the Bay

4536 Ocean View Avenue, Virginia Beach, Virginia
757-464-4999

BUSINESS SEASON: all year
HOURS: open daily for dinner
WATERVIEW: Chesapeake Bay
CREDIT CARDS: AE, DC, Disc, MC, Visa
HOUSE SPECIALTIES: broiled seafood combination platter, grilled salmon, prime rib of beef, Chesapeake Bay tournedos, oysters rockefeller, jumbo Gulf shrimp, tuna Norfolk, stuffed shrimp, duck à l'orange

When you find a seafood house where the fish is always fresh, the surroundings always congenial, and the staff always attentive and pleasant, you stick with it, and that's just what I've done since discovering Alexander's on the Bay.

The restaurant is a charmer, from the cool, contemporary decor to the magnificent Bay view. It offers food in the modern American style, beginning with clams casino, oysters Rockefeller, and bleu Bayou shrimp (jumbo Gulf shrimp filled with bleu cheese, wrapped in puff pastry). Entrées such as duck à l'orange—a generous portion of boneless duck breast fanned over a fabulous grand mariner sauce—and Alexander's tuna Norfolk—sautéed fresh yellow fin tuna steak capped with artichoke bottoms, backfin crab meat, and hollandaise sauce—are delectable. Among the better desserts is the flan au cognac. There's also a comprehensive list of premium wines by the glass.

Blue Crab

4521 Pretty Lake Avenue, Norfolk, Virginia
757-362-8000

BUSINESS SEASON: all year
HOURS: open daily for dinner
WATERVIEW: Little Creek/Chesapeake Bay
CREDIT CARDS: AE, MC, Visa
HOUSE SPECIALTIES: angels on horseback, shrimp Danish, oyster stew, grilled crab
   cakes, shrimp and scallop étouffée, braised tuna, pasta crusted salmon, tuna
   Norfolk, mussels Jacquelyn, Hatteras clam chowder

A cozy eatery with the old-time Norfolk atmosphere, this little cottage is a fun place
to spend a lazy evening. The food is good—from angels on horseback to oyster stew
to shrimp and scallop étouffée. The étouffée was one of the best I've ever tasted, and
when I mentioned it to owner Jim Perry, he told me, "It should be. It's Chef Paul
Prudhomme's personal recipe and it's made with a Virginia spicy andouille sausage."
My dish was chock full of tomatoes, green peppers, onions, and three ground peppers. It was hot! Chef Paul would be proud. Jim Perry, along with his wife Patty and
son Patrick, oversees the daily operation. On my last visit, I chose to sit at the tiny
bar. It was a good viewing point to watch the open kitchen as cooks tended to the
needs of customers. The Blue Crab has always been a place for everyone. While you're
there, it's easy to heed its advice, "Don't forget to have a good time."

The Ship's Cabin

4110 East Ocean View Avenue, Norfolk, Virginia
757-480-2526

BUSINESS SEASON: all year
HOURS: open daily for dinner only
WATERVIEW: Chesapeake Bay
CREDIT CARDS: AE, DC, MC, Visa
HOUSE SPECIALTIES: oysters bingo, slow grilled salmon, tuna mignon and stuffed
   shrimp, baked stuffed lobster, fresh catch, marinated chicken, fresh local soft-shells,
   crab cakes, summer vegetable crab soup, New York strip, fried green tomatoes

The Ship's Cabin is not an ordinary seafood restaurant. It reflects the bounty, romance, and magic of the sea. Simply put, it's one of the best 100 restaurants in America. The menu changes not just seasonally, not just weekly, but several times a week. Depending on what's available, what's fresh and what catches the creative fancy of the chef, a single evening may offer two dozen seafood entrées ranging from a simple, excellent grilled tuna mignon with a jumbo shrimp stuffed with fresh crab meat to fresh local soft-shell crabs sautéed and served with parmesan mashed potatoes, pesto, and a corn-pepper relish. The oyster bingo is always on the menu though—to prevent mutiny among the regular guests and ordered by Jimmy Buffet when he stops by. It's his favorite, and it may become yours, too.

Don't pass up the fried green tomatoes. It's a Southern tradition.

⑨
Fisherman's Wharf

1571 West Ocean View Avenue, Norfolk, Virginia
757-480-3113

BUSINESS SEASON: all year
HOURS: open daily for dinner; Thursday through Saturday for lunch and dinner
WATERVIEW: Hampton Creek/Hampton Roads Harbor
CREDIT CARDS: AE, DC, Disc, MC, Visa
HOUSE SPECIALTIES: world-famous seafood buffet plus fresh flounder, combination seafood platters, fried shrimp, baked crab, barbecued ribs, deviled crab, crab imperial, seafood au gratin, fried oysters, prime rib, shrimp Creole

There are two Fisherman's Wharf Restaurants. The other is across Hampton Roads in Hampton, Virginia. This one is an easy stroll from Willoughby Bay and Willoughby Harbor Marina. Once inside, you can't help but see the "World Famous Seafood Buffet," promoted as the "longest running buffet in Virginia." This could refer to the fact that the restaurant has featured this buffet since 1977, or to the sheer length of the buffet—it stretches to accommodate 75 items. I always order the buffet, making many trips to sample everything. First I choose fried scallops, oysters, chunky fried Gulf shrimp, baked bluefish, and a spicy deviled crab. On my next trip down the line, it's clam chowder and she-crab soup. Next I try the imperial crab, more fried oysters, and a small helping of seafood au gratin. I'm not done yet—I still have to taste the barbecued ribs and a slice of rare prime rib. Tantilizing breads and desserts offer a perfect finish.

10

O'Sullivan's Wharf

4300 Colley Avenue, Norfolk, Virginia
757-423-3746

BUSINESS SEASON: all year
HOURS: open daily for lunch and dinner
WATERVIEW: Lafayette River
CREDIT CARDS: AE, MC, Visa
HOUSE SPECIALTIES: fish of the day, shrimp tempura, crab cakes, the steamer, shrimp and scallop scampi, Capt. Sully's broiled combo, live lobster, Neptune's seafood combination platter, filet mignon, marinated chicken breast, steamed crabs

Sully's, as it is affectionately called by the locals and a handful of tourists, sits on an inconspicuous corner of 43rd Street and Colley Avenue. The parking lot tells the whole story: vintage cars driven by their original owners parked beside BMW's, beside pick-up trucks, beside foreign models. This is an honest place where you can get a great lunch at a fair price—a place where live jazz is played on the outdoor deck and you can sit and pick a steamed crab if you wish. It's also the best place for filet mignon—"The best cut in the Captain's Galley"—petite cut or Captain's cut—you decide. If you prefer a larger cut, it's available upon request. If you can't make up your mind, try the "indecisive"—a half dozen large shrimp alongside a handcut delmonico, petite filet, or prime rib. Sully's is a friendly place where your fellow diners could be families, business people, or ladies of the social set.

Phillips Waterside

333 Waterside Drive, Norfolk, Virginia
757-627-6600

BUSINESS SEASON: all year
HOURS: open daily for lunch and dinner
WATERVIEW: Elizabeth River
CREDIT CARDS: AE, DC, MC, Visa
HOUSE SPECIALTIES: crab and spinach dip, blue point oysters, crab mini's, she-crab soup, crab cakes, fresh catch, seafood linguine, shrimp and scallop sauté, seafood platter, baked stuffed shrimp, steak and shrimp combo

Phillips began as a carryout crab stand in Ocean City, Maryland, and has grown to nine restaurants throughout Maryland, Virginia, the District of Columbia, and Florida. In 1983, Phillips Waterside was opened, overlooking the Elizabeth River.

You may want to begin with the crab and spinach dip, served in a sourdough boule topped with mozzarella cheese. Another great starter is a plate of premium blue points harvested from the Long Island Sound, shucked cold and served on a bed of ice. Or the crab mini's—8 miniature crab cakes made with claw crab meat, fried golden brown and served with homemade tartar sauce. If you have the appetite to continue after the abundant appetizers, the spectacular entrées will set your tastebuds raving again. One of my favorite "Fresh Catch" choices is the oak roasted salmon—fresh salmon slow roasted on a real chardonnay oak barrel, served with dijon-dill beurre blanc.

12

The Max

425 Water Street, Portsmouth, Virginia
757-397-1866

BUSINESS SEASON: all year

HOURS: open Monday through Friday for lunch and dinner; Saturday, dinner only; closed Sunday

WATERVIEW: Elizabeth River

CREDIT CARDS: AE, Disc, MC, Visa

HOUSE SPECIALTIES: broiled seafood platter, Chicago-style prime rib, curry chicken or shrimp, herb-crusted salmon, lemon flounder, blackened seafood kabob, crab cakes

Portsmouth, across the Elizabeth River from downtown Norfolk, is a sleepy waterside community. In the heart of the quaint historic section is The Max, a cozy yet chic restaurant with uptown flair and lots of down-home personality. One of my favorite dishes is herb-crusted andouille chicken: a boneless, skinless chicken breast stuffed with andouille sausage and mozzarella cheese, then rolled in toasted, herb-flavored bread crumbs, broiled to a golden brown, and served on a bed of white sauce. Another is curry chicken or shrimp, described in the menu thus: "Our friend, Esmond Miranda, has shared with us a traditional recipe from his native country of India. Tender filets of chicken or chunks of tender shrimp folded into a bold curry, accompanied by rice and a side dish of yogurt with diced cucumbers and tomatoes to soothe the palate. Also served with pompaddums, the bread of India."

13

Amory's Wharf

10 Crawford Parkway, Portsmouth, Virginia
757-399-0991

BUSINESS SEASON: all year
HOURS: open daily for lunch and dinner
WATERVIEW: Elizabeth River
CREDIT CARDS: AE, MC, Visa
HOUSE SPECIALTIES: she-crab soup, bouillabaisse, crab cakes, scallops and shrimp in
    creamy alfredo sauce, fresh fish of the day, pan-seared lobster, seafood chef salad,
    steak and pasta specialties, oysters hollandaise

Amory's has been a major part of the Virginia seafood industry since the 1890's. For years the family has packed and shipped daily catches to seafood markets nationwide. Today, Amory's Wharf Seafood Restaurant is owned and operated by a member of the fourth generation—David Amory. Located at the Tidewater Yacht Club, it sits above the ship's store at the end of the pier on "B" dock. You have a great view from every direction, even at the bar, where mirrors reflect the glistening water. On a recent visit I began with the she-crab soup. The chef prides himself on creating everything from scratch, and this soup was a tasty example of his expertise! I also chose the crab cake and was surprised when my server asked, "Broiled, blackened, or fried?" It came with crisp cole slaw and roasted red potatoes. Not only is the food outstanding, the service is professional and particularly efficient.

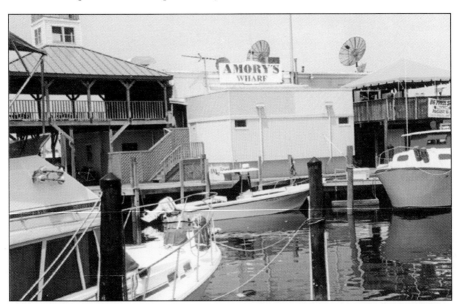

Scale O'De Whale

3515 Shipwright Street, Portsmouth, Virginia
757-483-2772

BUSINESS SEASON: all year

HOURS: open Monday through Friday for lunch and dinner; Saturday and Sunday for
dinner only

WATERVIEW: Elizabeth River

CREDIT CARDS: AE, DC, MC, Visa

HOUSE SPECIALTIES: stuffed tenderloin, seafood parmesan, flounder imperial, lemon
flounder, seafood pasta, veal oscar, blackened chicken, lobster tail

The Scale O'De Whale Restaurant has a well-deserved reputation as one of the finest
in the city. Its decor successfully combines refinement and comfort, and its obviously
well-trained staff is friendly and helpful. A taste of nearly any entrée on the menu
will make you a "Whale fan." The menu is rolled up like a treasure map, an appropriate way to present the delicious treasures of hosts Allison and Kouros Hamraz. The
menu features Hatteras clam chowder and she-crab soup and is full of seafood selections like "Neptune's Feast," a banquet for two: after soup or chowder, your host will
serve a large tossed salad smothered with your choice of dressing. Meanwhile the chef
will be preparing a combination plate of lobster, filet mignon, a stuffed shrimp, a loaf
of hot bread, a vegetable of your choice, and a glass of fine house wine. This sumptuous feast serves two.

15

Creekside Seafood Restaurant

3305 Ferry Road, Suffolk, Virginia
757-484-8700

BUSINESS SEASON: all year

HOURS: open daily for dinner; open Sunday for lunch and dinner

WATERVIEW: Bennett's Creek/Nansemond River

CREDIT CARDS: MC, Visa

HOUSE SPECIALTIES: seafood platter, shrimp stuffed with crab meat, crab cakes, grilled
tuna, grilled chicken breast, steamed shrimp, steamer combo, flounder stuffed with
crab meat, seafood pasta marinara, snowcrab legs

In its out-of-the-way location just outside Churchland, Creekside serves some of the
best local seafood in the area. Get there early, because the line forms about an hour
before opening. You'll delight in a new dining area that sits out over the water and
has floor to ceiling windows perfect for dining with a view. If you time your visit right,
you'll find delight in the soft crab shedding operation out on the pier.

The menu is abundant with seafood—my kind of place. One dish that has disappeared from many menus is crab cocktail. It's still here and it's excellent. There's
also crab salad, she-crab soup, and a creamy clam chowder, homemade and deliciously
thick. And when I want a great soft-shell crab sandwich or hush puppies, they're here,
too. Other favorites are the steamed shrimp, the crab cakes or the fresh flounder stuffed
with crab meat. This is the place to celebrate a special evening.

16

Smithfield Station

415 South Church Street, Smithfield, Virginia
757-357-7700

BUSINESS SEASON: all year
HOURS: open daily for lunch and dinner; open Saturday and Sunday for breakfast,
lunch, and dinner
WATERVIEW: Cypress Creek/Pagan River
CREDIT CARDS: AE, DC, Disc, MC, Visa
HOUSE SPECIALTIES: seafood platter, Norfolk combo, crab cakes, chicken Isle of Wight,
Smithfield surf & turf, Pagan River pork, Smithfield ham platter, pastas, beef, soups

Smithfield Station is the perfect place to watch the sun descend on the Pagan River. In the cedar-paneled dining room, every table offers a panorama of the River and marshes beyond. You'll want to sample seafood and specialty dishes unique to the area. For example, the Station's surf & turf combines succulent crab cakes with world-famous Smithfield ham. Smithfield is famous for its country hams, and the ham platter served here is to die for—baked to perfection, thinly sliced, and served with spiced apples. Owner Ron Pack slices the ham thin to give just enough of the salt taste and "just the right twang." Fresh flounder is offered broiled, fried, or Smithfield style—with crab meat, Smithfield ham, and béarnaise sauce. Another combination dinner I love is the Norfolk combo—crab meat, scallops, and shrimp cooked in garlic butter.

You'll find eating at Smithfield Station a uniquely memorable waterfront experience.

Dockside

700 Jordan Point Road, Hopewell, Virginia
804-541-2600

BUSINESS SEASON: all year
HOURS: open daily for lunch and dinner
WATERVIEW: James River
CREDIT CARDS: AE, MC, Visa
HOUSE SPECIALTIES: fresh broiled seafood, fresh fried seafood, whole Maine lobster, crab cakes, New York strip, Italian specialties, pasta, prime rib of beef au jus, stuffed mushrooms with imperial crab meat

Dockside Restaurant is near the Shirley Plantation, home of Robert E. Lee's mother, Anne Hill Carter. Today, the plantation is home to the ninth and tenth generations of the Hill-Carter Family. You'll enjoy a tour of the property where Washington, Jefferson, and countless other prominent Americans were entertained. When it's time for *you* to be entertained, stop at the Dockside for dinner, a lovely round cedar structure on a bluff overlooking the James River. The cuisine favors seafood, with some Italian dishes thrown in. Appetizers include stuffed mushrooms with imperial crab meat sautéed in wine and garlic butter and spanakopita—baked spinach and cheese wrapped in filo. For dinner, the Italian specialties include delicious manicotti, lasagna, and spaghettini. The broiled, stuffed flounder laced with a spiced crab meat mix also gets top marks, along with lobster, crab, and steaks—and don't forget the key lime pie for dessert.

18

Captain's Cove

910 North 21st Street, Hopewell, Virginia
804-452-1368

BUSINESS SEASON: all year
HOURS: open daily for lunch and dinner
WATERVIEW: confluence of the Appomattox and James Rivers
CREDIT CARDS: AE, DC
HOUSE SPECIALTIES: the Steam-it Platter, Fisherman's Feast, shrimp Norfolk scampi,
   t-bone steak, southern fried chicken, seafood stir-fry, cream of crab soup, chicken
   breast sautée, barbecue shrimp, pasta primavera

As it flows near the western border of Virginia to the Chesapeake Bay, the 450-mile-long James River carries with it a rich history. Sir Thomas Dale laid out a settlement in 1614 named "Bermuda Cittie," (later changed to City Point, and later yet to Hopewell), in a magnificent location on the bluff overlooking the confluence of the Appomatox and James rivers. For more history, study the back of the Captain's Cove menu after placing your order.

For starters, try the barbecued shrimp wrapped in bacon, and follow that with the Cove's cream of crab soup. If you enjoy a seafood and pasta combination, try the pasta primavera—tender seafood delicately prepared with a pasta and vegetable medley in a white or red sauce. And be sure to leave room for dessert. You'll savor the hot fudge cake or gourmet cheesecake with a fruit topping.

8: About the Virginia Peninsula

Pirates, pioneers, and some of history's most intriguing personalities have called the Virginia Peninsula home. Captain John Smith stopped here in 1607 on the way to Jamestown. In the early 1700s, Blackbeard lay in wait for his unwary victims. In 1781, the British under Cornwallis surrendered to the allied Americans and French forces at Yorktown in the last major battle of the American Revolution. In the 1950s, Mercury astronauts rehearsed in Hampton, Virginia for their historic blast into the space age.

Today the world-famous Mariner's Museum celebrated the spirit of seafaring adventure with an international collection of handcrafted ship models, paintings, figureheads, steam engines and vintage small craft. Visitors to the region will be impressed with its historical atmosphere but also with its cuisine. Be prepared to savor carefully prepared dishes in the most charming surroundings—with a view of the water.

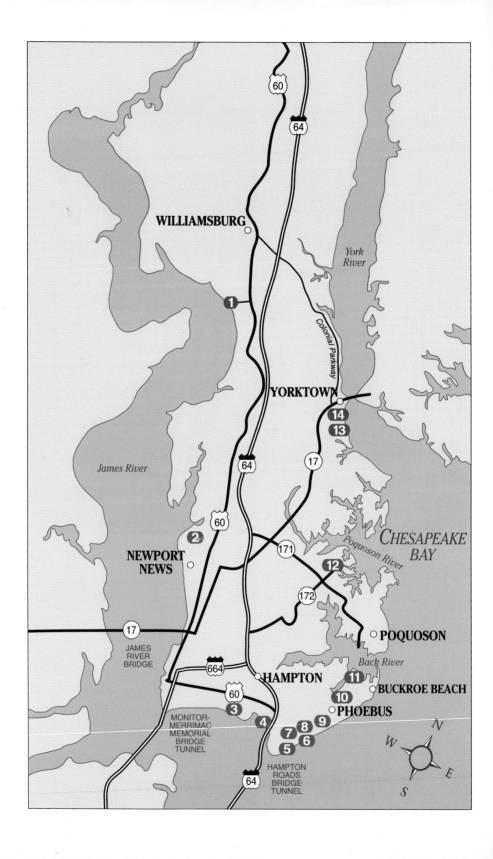

Virginia Peninsula Waterside Dining

INCLUDES: Williamsburg, Newport News, Hampton, Fort Monroe
Phoebus, Buckroe Beach, Poquoson, and Yorktown, Virginia.

1. The Bray Dining Room
2. Herman's Harbor House
3. Fisherman's Wharf
4. The View
5. Chamberlin Hotel Restaurant
6. Eller's on the Bay
7. Victor's Restaurant
8. Oyster Alley
9. Keith's Dockside
10. Sam's Seafood Restaurant
11. Buckroe Island Grill
12. Bubba's Ships Galley
13. Yorktown Pub
14. Nick's Seafood Pavilion

The Bray Dining Room

100 Kingsmill Road, Williamsburg, Virginia
757-253-1703

BUSINESS SEASON: all year

HOURS: open daily, breakfast, lunch, and dinner

WATERVIEW: James River

CREDIT CARDS: AE, DC, Disc, MC, Visa

HOUSE SPECIALTIES: seafood stew, filet mignon, rack of lamb, crab cakes, roast
bobwhite quail, grilled fresh salmon, marinated veal chops, seared and slow roasted
muscovy duck

In 1972, the erosion of a portion of the James River's bank revealed a 250-year-old
secret: a 17th-century well shaft. Upon excavation by archaeologists from the Virginia
Historic Landmarks Commission, this shaft provided evidence of significant findings
located on the Kingsmill property and led to the establishment of the Kingsmill
Archaeological Project.

The treasure *you'll* discover at the Bray Dining Room is the culinary talent of
Executive Chef Joseph Durante. His signature crab cake, presented with gunpowder
aioli and fresh fennel grapefruit relish, ranks among the world's best. (I've sampled
many!) If filet mignon is your choice, it comes grilled to perfection with a complex-
ity of vegetables and lattice potatoes, ready to be enjoyed with a roast shallot merlot
sauce.

②
Herman's Harbor House

663 Deep Creek Road, Newport News, Virginia
757-930-1000

BUSINESS SEASON: all year
HOURS: open Sunday through Friday for lunch and dinner; Saturday for dinner only
WATERVIEW: Deep Creek/James River
CREDIT CARDS: AE, MC, Visa
HOUSE SPECIALTIES: oysters and clams on the half shell, she-crab soup, clam chowder, seafood chowder, crab cakes, fried oysters, soft-shell crabs, imperial crab, shrimp/scallop/or crab meat au gratin, stuffed shrimp, Captain Wyndham's gourmet platter

Of all the dining choices one may have in the Newport News area, there are few, if any, that can compare to the excellent cuisine and service found at Herman's Harbor House. All of the seafood is carefully selected by Herman, whose family has a century of seafood harvesting and processing behind them, so you can be assured that every effort is made to serve you the very freshest seafood.

My favorite is the Norfolk combo: Gulf shrimp, crab meat, scallops, and chunks of lobster sautéed in hot garlic butter and seasoned with fresh herbs. It sounds good, and it tastes even better than it sounds. Another favorite is Captain Wyndham's Gourmet Platter. It begins with a cup of fresh clam chowder and a fresh salad. Then oysters and clams on the half shell, rock lobster, crab imperial, Gulf shrimp, sea scallops and filet of flounder. Caution: This is only for a ravenous appetite.

Fisherman's Wharf

14 Ivy Home Road, Hampton, Virginia
757-723-3113

BUSINESS SEASON: all year

HOURS: open Monday through Friday for dinner only; Saturday and Sunday for lunch and dinner

WATERVIEW: Hampton Creek/Hampton Roads Harbor

CREDIT CARDS: AE, MC, Visa

HOUSE SPECIALTIES: seafood buffet (the longest running in Virginia), steamed shrimp, shrimp creole, fried select oysters, broiled fish, she-crab soup, seafood au gratin

Newport News is a city of the sea, boasting a premier seaport and shipbuilding facility, both located along the world's largest natural harbor. If you want to enjoy great seafood, I suggest you visit Fisherman's Wharf Restaurant, "the home of the original world famous seafood buffet." Here is just a sampler from the 75 items offered on my last visit: baked whole fish, steamed blue crabs, New England clam chowder, she-crab soup, fried ocean clam strips, steamed shrimp (boy, were they good!), steamed mussels, broiled bluefish, fried select oysters, blueberry muffins, cornbread, hush puppies, tuna salad, crab salad, buttered broccoli, parsley-buttered potatoes, cut green beans, corn on the cob, banana pudding, cherry cobbler, Black Forest cake, carrot cake, watermelon basket ... and more, much, much more!

You may run into me the next time you're there!

④
The View

Strawberry Banks Lane, Hampton, Virginia
757-723-6061

BUSINESS SEASON: all year

HOURS: open daily for breakfast, lunch, and dinner

WATERVIEW: Hampton Roads Harbor

CREDIT CARDS: AE, DC, Disc, MC, Visa

HOUSE SPECIALTIES: surf & turf, seafood platter, veal chops, chicken with wild mushrooms, New York strip, crab cakes, tuna Mardi Gras, chicken alfredo, shrimp scampi, angels on horseback, steamed clams

The View dining room is a part of the Strawberry Banks Inn. Surrounded by the timeless beauty of the Chesapeake Bay, this ideal vacation spot boasts over 32 acres of gardens for jogging, a beach for walking, and a fishing pier.

The restaurant and outdoor patio overlook the harbor and present the finest in dining. During my latest visit, I savored Chef Billee Watkins' stuffed Portobello mushrooms—stuffed jumbo shrimp enveloped in the mushrooms with roasted garlic, tomatoes and Muenster cheese. This dish came with The View's Wow Salad—crisp greens topped with roasted peppers, tomatoes, egg, and sliced olives, fried potatoes and red onion. You can have your salad with blackened chicken or steak, and it really deserves the title "Wow"! I completed my meal with a dozen top neck clams served with drawn butter and then retired to a lounge chair for a nap before I searched out my next meal.

Chamberlin Hotel Restaurant

Old Point Comfort, Fort Monroe, Virginia
757-723-6511, ext. 168

BUSINESS SEASON: all year
HOURS: open daily for breakfast, lunch, and dinner
WATERVIEW: Hampton Roads/Chesapeake Bay
CREDIT CARDS: AE, DC, MC, Visa
HOUSE SPECIALTIES: shrimp cocktail, stuffed mushrooms, Chesapeake clam chowder, Virginia breast of chicken, Chamberlin crab cakes, mixed grill, New York strip, stuffed flounder, shrimp scampi, chef's special offering of the day

At the Chamberlin Hotel at Hampton's Old Point Comfort, the huge windows overlooking Hampton Roads Harbor creates a feeling of pre-World War II dining splendor. The Hampton Room won't disappoint you; it captures the carefree, luxurious spirit and romantic ambience of days long past.

One of my favorite starter courses in the Hampton Room is the shrimp cocktail. Five jumbo shrimp ring a bowl of ice and are accompanied by fresh lemons and a delightful sauce. Although lighter entrées are available as well as steaks and chops, I always head for the seafood side of the menu. In the past I've enjoyed the Chamberlin's crab cake dinner, featuring cakes made from the finest backfin crab and then broiled. But on my last visit, I tried, and loved, something different—the mixed grill: scallops, shrimp, flounder and—surprise—a crab cake! It was marvelous.

⑥
Eller's on the Bay

107 McNair Drive, Fort Monroe, Virginia
757-722-2487

BUSINESS SEASON: all year
HOURS: open daily for lunch and dinner
WATERVIEW: Chesapeake Bay
CREDIT CARDS: AE, DC, MC, Visa
HOUSE SPECIALTIES: James River crab cakes, Poquoson soft-shell crab dinner, fried
Chincoteague oysters, Outer Banks shrimp, blackened catfish, Tidewater broiled
platter, crab meat Hampton, steak and seafood platters

I can't tell you how many times I've passed by Eller's on the Bay and always thought
it was a marina—it never dawned on me that it was a restaurant! It was only by chance
that I learned of this new (to me) eating adventure. A stairway at bayside leads to the
second floor restaurant, where nautical photographs and posters and polished dark
wood complement the hunter green decor. A rambunctious bar dominates one side
of the dining room and a wall of windows lets in plenty of light.

The beer battered shrimp I chose from a long list of appetizers were large, hot,
and fried just right. I wanted to try the James River crab cakes, but unfortunately
they were sold out, so I ordered the Poquoson soft-shell crab dinner instead—three
locally harvested crabs, a heaping pile of hush puppies, and a generous portion of creamy
cole slaw. Now that I've found this place, I'm going back!

Victor's Restaurant
700 Settlers Landing Road, Hampton, Virginia
757-727-9700

BUSINESS SEASON: all year
HOURS: open daily for breakfast, lunch, and dinner
WATERVIEW: Hampton River
CREDIT CARDS: AE, DC, Disc, MC, Visa
HOUSE SPECIALTIES: Key lime seafood pasta, poached halibut, shrimp parmesan, Hampton crab cakes, classic Caesar salad, Shenandoah pork loin, New York strip steak, Caribbean-style grouper

The Radisson Hotel Hampton, is in the heart of space exploration country and is the home of Victor's Restaurant. Adjacent to it is the Virginia Air and Space Center and Carousel Park, and not far away is NASA's Langley Research Center, where America's first astronauts, the Mercury Seven, were trained.

Chef Ray Garrow proudly presents exciting new menu selections with appetizing appeal. Take, for example, the fire-grilled Shenandoah Pork Loin in a bourbon sauce served with shoestring sweet potatoes and an apple pecan compote. Or how about the Chesapeake Seafood Symphony, a combination of Gulf shrimp, sea scallops, and fresh fish with a lemon butter sauce, served with a wild rice flan! It's music to my palate.

Once you try Victor's, you'll agree that even in space exploration country you don't have to leave the ground to find food that's out of this world!

8

Oyster Alley

700 Settlers Landing Road, Hampton, Virginia
757-727-9700

BUSINESS SEASON: April 1 to October 1
HOURS: open daily for lunch and dinner, weather permitting
WATERVIEW: Hampton River
CREDIT CARDS: AE, DC, Disc, MC, Visa
HOUSE SPECIALTIES: crab cake sandwich, pulled pork barbecue sandwich, mahi-mahi
  sandwich, poached salmon salad, shrimp Caesar salad, oysters on the half shell,
  stuffed roasted oysters

Hampton's scenic harbor—Front City—is a great place to visit and eplore. Located a few steps from the Visitor's Center is the Hampton Carousel, a restored 1920s merry-go-round, a rare piece of American Folk Art. After spending more than 65 years at Hampton's Buckroe Beach Amusement Park, the carousel was restored and moved to its new home on the downtown waterfront.

A few steps in the other direction is Oyster Alley, which is a part of the Radisson Hotel Hampton Complex. Your first glimpse of it will be a long green awning and beautiful potted flowers that dominate the scene. Oyster Alley is not fancy, but it's fun. I love to sit here on the waterfront, slurp a dozen raw oysters, and drink a cold beer or two. Whether your Hampton visit is for a day or "days on end," I know you'll end up at Oyster Alley.

9
Keith's Dockside

38-C Water Street, Phoebus, Virginia
757-723-1781

BUSINESS SEASON: all year
HOURS: open daily for lunch and dinner
WATERVIEW: Mill Creek/Hampton Roads
CREDIT CARDS: AE, DC, Disc, MC, Visa
HOUSE SPECIALTIES: dockside platter (mixed seafood), crab soup, crab cakes, mixed
   crab platter, sautéed backfin crab meat, shrimp basket, steamed shrimp, broiled
   scallops, baked stuffed flounder with imperial crab, chargrilled swordfish steak

Keith Brown opened Keith's Dockside restaurant in 1974 and has a strong local following—he wouldn't have been in business this long without it. Back in the time of Prohibition, this tiny waterfront town had a saloon on every corner, but they've all disappeared and renovation is on the rise in the area. One thing I hope never changes is the food served at Keith's Dockside.

Along with Keith's world-famous crab soup and crab cake is the Dockside platter. You may choose three items from this list: flounder, oysters, shrimp, crab cake, clam strips, scallops, soft crab (seasonal) and steamed shrimp. This delightful platter is served with slaw, choice of potato and hush puppies. Now hush, you hear? I don't want too many folks to find out about Keith's Dockside!

Sam's Seafood Restaurant

23 Water Street, Phoebus, Virginia
757-723-3709

BUSINESS SEASON: all year

HOURS: open daily for lunch and dinner

WATERVIEW: Mill Creek/Hampton Roads

CREDIT CARDS: AE, MC, Visa

HOUSE SPECIALTIES: fried seafood, broiled seafood, seafood sautéed, steak, oyster stew, clam chowder, Cap't Sam's crab meat and clam chowder, seafood pasta, mariner's seafood platter

The history of the military in Hampton Roads can be traced to Colonial times. This great harbor drew early explorers to the area. In 1609, just two years after the arrival of the first English settlers, a fort was built on the present site of Fort Monroe, today's headquarters for the U.S. Army Training and Doctrine Command.

When the folks stationed at Fort Monroe want to get away from mess hall fare, they cross the Causeway and head for Sam's—and like them, once you've eaten there, you'll be back. You'll find flounder stuffed with lump crab meat, broiled to perfection and rushed to your table. If you're really hungry, try Sam's deluxe platter: crab cake, three huge shrimp, scallops, clam strips and flounder. There's much more, but you'll find that out yourself. You won't be disappointed!

Buckroe Island Grill

One Ivory Gull Crescent, Buckroe Beach, Virginia
757-850-5757

BUSINESS SEASON: all year

HOURS: open daily for lunch and dinner

WATERVIEW: Back River

CREDIT CARDS: AE, DC, Disc, MC, Visa

HOUSE SPECIALTIES: catch of the day, lemon pepper tuna, filet mignon, seafood burrito, crab cake dinner, blackened shrimp tortellini, Eastern Shore clams and Gulf oysters, chicken quesadilla, catch of the day

According to *Signposts and Settlers* by Robert I. Alotta, one tale about Buckroe Beach "has it that Frenchmen sent over to this continent in 1620 to plant mulberry trees and grape vines settled here." Records dating to 1617 call the area Buck Row. There was a plantation on the site that drew its name from Buckrose, Yorkshire, England.

Today if you want a great place to relax, try the clean sand, gentle surf, and lively summer band concerts of Hampton's Buckroe Beach. Also lively is the Buckroe Island Grill, in the talented hands of Chef Mo Mzil, a talented chap with a tremendous following around the area. The Grill's menu is short but tasty and includes the day's catch that you can order grilled or blackened. Next time you're there, try it with Walkerswood jerk topped with sautéed backfin or grilled with lemon pepper seasoning.

12

Bubba's Ships Galley Restaurant

105 Rens Road, Poquoson, Virginia
757-868-7980

BUSINESS SEASON: all year
HOURS: open daily for breakfast, lunch, and dinner
WATERVIEW: White House Cove/Poquoson River
CREDIT CARDS: MC, Visa
HOUSE SPECIALTIES: surf and turf, steamed shrimp platter, soft crab platter, flounder
  platter, clam strips, six- or ten-ounce steak, fried oyster platter, soft-shell crab
  platter, clam chowder

Bubba's Ships Galley is located at Bull Island Marina on White House Cove on the
Poquoson River. Poquoson has been spelled many ways through the years, including
Pocosin and Pokoson, but it's always been pronounced *po-KO-son,* and the people who
live there are known as "Poquosonites" or sometimes "Bull Islanders."

As you drive up to Bubba's you'll know immediately why it's called the Ships Galley:
It's a large work boat that has been converted into a landlocked eatery, and its location next to the boat ramp is one reason why it's so successful. I recommend these
three entrées, each available fried or steamed: the Captain's Platter, which includes
shrimp, clams, scallops, fish and a crab cake; the Mate's Platter, featuring shrimp, scallops, clams, and fish; and the Galley's Surf and Turf, a six-ounce steak, a quarter pound
of shrimp, and a quarter pound of scallops.

⑬

Yorktown Pub

540 Water Street, Yorktown, Virginia
no phone

BUSINESS SEASON: all year
HOURS: open daily for lunch and dinner
WATERVIEW: York River
CREDIT CARDS: none
HOUSE SPECIALTIES: oysters on the half shell, Yorktown clam chowder, fried fish
   sandwich, broiled scallops, marinated prime rib, reuben on rye, pub burger, fried
   soft-shell crab sandwich, peanut butter and jelly sandwich with chips

The land on which Yorktown was built was patented by a French engineer in 1630.
The Virginia Assembly authorized the establishment of a port here in 1680. On October 19, 1781, the British under Cornwallis surrendered to the allied American and
French forces here in what was to become the last major battle of the American
Revolution. Today in Yorktown it's fun to view the scenic York River, just minutes
from the battlefield where independence was won. The front door opens onto the
most historic beach in America today.

   The restaurant attracts a younger clientele and exudes a down-home atmosphere.
On my last visit, dinner at the Yorktown Pub was pure delight. I started with a dozen
oysters on the half shell. Those oysters were so good I then selected a dozen more of
them steamed.

Nick's Seafood Pavilion

Water Street, Yorktown, Virginia
757-887-5269

BUSINESS SEASON: all year

HOURS: open daily for lunch and dinner

WATERVIEW: York River

CREDIT CARDS: AE, DC, MC, Visa

HOUSE SPECIALTIES: soft-shell crabs sautéed in butter, crab cakes, broiled lobster tail, french-fried jumbo shrimp, broiled pork tenderloin, Grecian baked oysters à la casino, catch of the day

Ψ Y & ☎

Yorktown, Jamestown and Williamsburg form Virginia's "Historic Triangle," a region that had a major role in the creation of our country. The Yorktown Victory Center, a museum of the American Revolution, is an exceptional place to taste the historical flavor of the area, and Nick's Seafood Pavilion is a fantastic place to taste the area's seafood delights.

Just entering Nick's is an experience. Once you've strolled through a Greek garden, complete with statues of ancient gods, water gardens and exotic lighting, you'll find yourself in a large dining room dominated by a gigantic chandelier.

The food is as exceptional as the atmosphere. You'll find many Greek dishes, from broiled quail to broiled tenderloin, but Nick's specializes in its preparation of shrimp, crab and lobster. And don't miss the catch of the day—always fresh and delicious!

9: About the Northern Neck & Middle Peninsula

Nature, boating, history, fishing, and recreation are all a part of this area. Many parts of the York and Rappahannock rivers and their tributaries are much as they were when the Powhatan Indians first hunted wild game and fished along their shores. It was at the mouth of the Rappahannock in 1607 that Captain John Smith, while spearing for fish, nearly succumbed to poisoning by a sting ray.

On the Northern Neck, you're never more than a few miles from water, and a boat tour is a must if you want a real taste of the Chesapeake lifestyle. Then round out your visit with a meal at one of the restaurants in this chapter, where chefs spend time in the kitchen preparing the finest, freshest foods with skill and care ... while you spend time enjoying the water view!

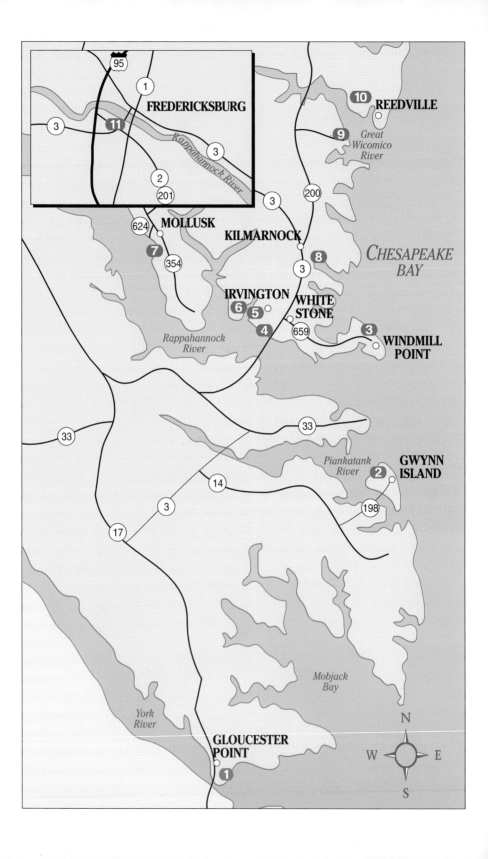

Northern Neck and Middle Peninsula Waterside Dining

INCLUDES: Gloucester Point, Gwynn Island, Windmill Point, White Stone, Irvington, Mollusk, Kilmarnock, Burgess, Reedville and Fredericksburg, Virginia

1. River's Inn Restaurant
2. The Golden Anchor
3. The Front Porch
4. Annabel Lee
5. Tides Inn
6. Tides Lodge
7. The Upper Deck Restaurant
8. The Crab Shack
9. Horn Harbor House
10. Elijah's Restaurant
11. The Riverview

❶
River's Inn Restaurant

8109 Yacht Haven Drive, Gloucester Point, Virginia
804-642-9942

BUSINESS SEASON: all year
HOURS: open daily for lunch and dinner
WATERVIEW: Sarah's Creek/York River
CREDIT CARDS: AE, MC, Visa
HOUSE SPECIALTIES: blackened fresh dolphin, fresh whole lobster, Chesapeake Bay "Blue Plate," bouillabaisse, pan-fried crab cake with Surry Ham, fresh soft-shell crabs, steamed crabs, grilled filet mignon, baked oysters

This area of the Gloucester Point shore belonged chiefly to nearby plantations until after World War I. A ferry traversed the short distance from Yorktown to Gloucester Point during most of Virginia's existence. At the entrance to Sarah's Creek is the York River Yacht Haven Marina, home to the River's Inn Restaurant. It's a new dining spot that already has a great following. The decor is nautical and there are plenty of windows from which you can view pleasure yachts and fishing boats.

A knockout specialty of the River's Inn is fried fresh Virginia oysters with country ham and caramelized onion sauce, whipped sweet potatoes and sliced Hanover tomatoes. The chef's pan-fried deviled crab cake with Surry ham, tomatoes, Boston lettuce and spicy Thousand Island dressing is also a big hit, and the deck and screened pavilion are perfect spots to enjoy a dozen or so hot steamed crabs—usually my choice!

②

The Golden Anchor

Old Ferry Road, Gwynns Island, Virginia
804-725-2151

BUSINESS SEASON: Memorial Day to Labor Day
HOURS: open daily for lunch and dinner
WATERVIEW: Milford Haven/Piankatank River
CREDIT CARDS: Disc, MC, Visa
HOUSE SPECIALTIES: Virginia crab cake, baked imperial crab, fried jumbo shrimp, snow crab clusters, stuffed filet of fish, baked stuffed shrimp, iron kettle clam chowder, New York strip sirloin steak

Legend holds that Colonel Hugh Gwynn was given this island in gratitude for helping rescue the daughter of a Piankatank chief from a capsized canoe. It's fun to cross the swing bridge and walk or drive through the island, which retains the flavor of a turn-of-the century fishing village. At the western tip is the Islander at Narrows Marina—the home of the Golden Anchor Restaurant.

The Golden Anchor's variety and prices are some of the best you'll find. The feature is "Barnacle Bill"—fresh Virginia crab meat mixed with spices, molded in cakes, lightly dusted with breadcrumbs and fried to perfection (or broiled if you wish). Another favorite is baked imperial crab "Chesapeake"—a blend of snow-white crab meat and a carefully seasoned sauce. The view over the lighted pool to the river beyond is entrancing any time of day and the service is friendly and efficient.

❸
The Front Porch

Route 695, Windmill Point, Virginia
804-435-1166

BUSINESS SEASON: April through November
HOURS: open daily for lunch and dinner
WATERVIEW: Rappahannock River
CREDIT CARDS: AE, MC, Visa
HOUSE SPECIALTIES: roast pork tenderloin, grilled bacon-wrapped oysters, fried oysters,
  beef burgundy, black Angus filet mignon, lemon shallot chicken, honey pecan
  chicken breast, pan-fried bay scallops, soft-shell crabs, hot crab dip, crab bisque

If you're looking for a place to "get away from it all," but want to do it in style, there's
no better choice than Windmill Point, located at the confluence of the Rappahannock
River and the Chesapeake Bay. The Point is a fine little resort blessed with one of the
Chesapeake's most beautiful locations. It offers beachfront rooms with wonderful views,
tennis, golf, rental boats, fishing, swimming, bicycling, hiking, and a mile of sand beach.

The Front Porch Restaurant is the spot for fine dining at the Point, featuring seafood
as well as dishes with a continental touch. Have you ever had Angels on Horseback?
This Front Porch special is fresh oysters on a skewer wrapped in wafer-thin bacon
and broiled to a golden brown—incredible! Other specials like the honey pecan chicken
breast and soft-shell crabs fried or broiled to your order are equally marvelous. And
if you still have room, don't miss the hot brownie sundae with toasted almonds.

❹
Annabel Lee

327 Old Ferry Road, White Stone, Virginia
804-435-7378

BUSINESS SEASON: all year

HOURS: open Tuesday through Sunday for dinner only; closed Mondays

WATERVIEW: Rappahannock River

CREDIT CARDS: MC, Visa

HOUSE SPECIALTIES: prime rib, filet mignon, t-bone, broiled marinated chicken breast, crab imperial, crab cake dinner, shrimp scampi, broiled salmon, cracker and crab dip, veal scallopini, seafood bisque

The Annabel Lee is built in the style of a paddle wheel ferry boat that once transported travelers and goods across the lower Rappahannock. It didn't start out as a restaurant—it was built as a motel to house the workers that worked on the bridge that replaced the ferry. A reminder of more civilized and structured times, the Annabel Lee oozes charm … from the Topside Lounge to the panoramic view of the Rappahannock from the lower level.

In the restaurant, you'll find traditional American food. Prime rib is a favorite of many, with subtle, rather than overwhelming flavor. Steaks are also popular, and the seafood, whether it's soft-shell crabs, broiled salmon, or shrimp scampi served over pasta, keeps visitors coming back for more.

⑤
The Tides Inn

Irvington, Virginia
804-438-5000

BUSINESS SEASON: March 19 to January 3
HOURS: open daily for breakfast, lunch, and dinner
WATERVIEW: Carter Creek/Rappahannock River
CREDIT CARDS: AE, Disc, DC, MC, Visa
HOUSE SPECIALTIES: pan-fried native soft-shell crabs, shrimp stuffed with native crab meat, fresh poached salmon, flounder topped with shrimp and pecans, stuffed cornish hen, sliced beef tenderloin, hot fudge ice cream puff

It's a pleasure to experience the graciousness and personalized attention to detail found at the Tides Inn resort and dining facilities—perhaps the only inn with its own antique yacht, the 127-foot *Miss Ann*, available for dinner cruises and afternoon crabfeast excursions to the Inn's private beach on Windmill Point.

Executive chef Ken Barber oversees the Inn's three restaurants: the 320-seat main dining room; Commodore's, an informal 200-seat eatery near the pool; and Captain B's, an 80-seat facility at the golf course. The main dining room rotates four menus in addition to a Sunday seafood buffet. Here's a sampler of entrées from a June evening: pan-seared rib eye steak, roast loin of pork, grilled fresh swordfish, seafood Norfolk en croute, marinated chicken breast, and pan-fried native soft-shell crabs with vegetables, fresh-baked bread, and delicious desserts. Save room. This place is special.

6
The Tides Lodge

One St. Andrews Land, Irvington, Virginia
804-438-6000

BUSINESS SEASON: mid-March to December
HOURS: open daily for lunch and dinner
WATERVIEW: Carter Creek/Rappahannock River
CREDIT CARDS: Disc, MC, VISA
HOUSE SPECIALTIES: fresh clams or oysters (steamed or on the half shell), seafood
  bisque, shrimp and lobster bisque, stuffed flounder, baked yellow fin tuna, broiled
  catfish filets, broiled orange roughy, crab cakes

Irvington was settled by John Carter in 1649. In the early days it was home to most of Virginia's first families, and today it's the home of some of the most prestigious yachting facilities in the Middle Atlantic area.

You'll enjoy a visit to historic Christ Church, built in 1732, the year of George Washington's birth and one of the outstanding examples of colonial churches in Virginia. A stone's throw from the church is the Tides Lodge, where you'll be treated to a beautiful view of Carter Creek while you dine in the Royal Stewart dining room or the informal Binnacle, with its panoramic view. Every item is prepared to order, and you can choose from baked flounder filets stuffed with crab meat, clams, oysters on the half shell, or shrimp and lobster bisque. You'll feel like an honored guest at a sophisticated private home here; it's a delightful experience.

The Upper Deck Restaurant

Route 624, Mollusk, Virginia
804-462-7400

BUSINESS SEASON: March through November, Friday and Saturday only; Memorial Day through Labor Day Thursday through Saturday

HOURS: open daily from 4:30 PM to 9 PM

WATERVIEW: Greenvale Creek/Rappahannock River

CREDIT CARDS: none

HOUSE SPECIALTIES: seafood buffet (it's super), crab cakes, crab au gratin, crab imperial, steaks, fried chicken, liver and onions, boiled scallops, Virginia ham

Milton and Gayle Conrad opened the Upper Deck Restaurant in April 1986 on top of the Old Oyster House. The downstairs, under the name of E.J. Conrad and Sons Seafood, is local favorite. Upstairs, where Milton took over from his dad, who was a waterman, is a small pine-paneled restaurant with many ceiling fans.

The Upper Deck offers no menu, but features a seafood buffet and daily specials. A blackboard posted outside lists the day's offerings. My lucky catch was fried oysters, spiced shrimp, crab balls, broiled fish, crab legs, salad bar, potato salad, cole slaw, shrimp salad, fruit salad, and clam chowder.

After dinner, take time to walk down to the waterside and enjoy the view of picturesque Greenvale Creek.

8

The Crab Shack

Route 672, Kilmarnock, Virginia
804-435-2700

BUSINESS SEASON: March through December
HOURS: open Tuesday through Sunday for lunch and dinner; closed Mondays
WATERVIEW: Indian Creek/Chesapeake Bay
CREDIT CARDS: AE, Disc, MC, Visa
HOUSE SPECIALTIES: crab salad, steamed crabs, crab meat cocktail, crab dip, seafood
platter, crab cake, fish of the day, stuffed flounder, stuffed shrimp, royal beef and
reef, crab imperial, scallops, spiced shrimp, soft-shell crabs

The New World Dictionary describes *shack* as "a small house or cabin that is crudely built." Although the Crab Shack's exterior is nondescript, the interior is comfortable and attractive. Owner Charles Chase expanded the already very popular Seafood Market into this restaurant with indoor and deck dining. (The Seafood Market still specializes in fresh crab meat, scallops, shrimp, fish, homemade crab cake, deviled crabs and crab salads for you to carry home.)

Lots of jovial conversation among the frequent local visitors gives the Shack a friendly, familiar atmosphere—you'll find that everyone seems to know everyone else. They keep coming back for the Shack's superior seafood and steaks. In addition to the specialties listed above, check the blackboard for daily lunch and dinner specials ... and the gorgeous sunsets are free!

Horn Harbor House

Route 810, Burgess, Virginia
804-453-3351

BUSINESS SEASON: April through November

HOURS: open Wednesday through Monday for dinner only; closed Tuesdays

WATERVIEW: Great Wicomico River

CREDIT CARDS: none

HOUSE SPECIALTIES: lobster tail, fried or broiled seafood platter, crab cake, select
oysters, seafood au gratin, crab meat au gratin, cold seafood sampler, spaghetti
Chesapeake, seafood bisque, clam chowder, spiced steamed shrimp

Horn Harbor, located about three miles above Sandy Point on the Great Wicomico
River, is something special. This snug hurricane hole is home to the Horn Harbor
Restaurant at the Great Wicomico Marina. This is an intimate little jewel of a place
where owners Kathy and Buddy Becker treat loyal patrons and first-time visitors to superb
home-cooked seafood.

Classic Chesapeake seafood is the style here, with some interesting twists: try the
Spaghetti Chesapeake baked in a red clam sauce and topped with shrimp and two
cheeses or Seafood Norfolk—your choice of seafood sautéed in lemon and butter. My
favorite dish is the crab meat au gratin—fresh backfin crab meat baked in a light cheese
sauce. If you have a large appetite, try the Horn Harbor Steamboat: steamed lobster
tail, crab, clams, shrimp and crab legs.

10

Elijah's Restaurant

Main Street, Reedville, Virginia
804-453-3621

BUSINESS SEASON: all year
HOURS: Open Wednesday through Sunday for lunch and dinner; closed Mondays and
  Tuesdays
WATERVIEW: Cockrell Creek/Great Wicomico River
CREDIT CARDS: MC, Visa
HOUSE SPECIALTIES: bacon-wrapped scallops, seafood bisque, fresh baked salmon,
  shrimp over pasta, grilled ribeye, fresh herb roasted pork loin, chicken parmigiana

The history of Reedville can be traced back as far as 1874, when Elijah W. Reed, a
sea captain from Maine, began a fishing business. He was after menhaden, and the
menhaden fishery was one of the most important and productive on the Atlantic Coast.

Now, 123 years later, Elijah Reed's great-great-grandson, W. Taylor Slaughter, owns
Elijah's Restaurant in the renovated Blundon and Hinton Mercantile, built circa 1890
on the banks of Cockrell Creek. Here fresh seafood, prime cuts of beef, homemade
breads, desserts and wonderful salads are served in a casual atmosphere. I began with
a creamy lobster-laden seafood bisque that would have delighted any coastal waterman. Another popular entrée is scallops wrapped with bacon; they're gently broiled
and served with an aged sherry vinegar sauce. As you dine, keep in mind that Elijah
is never far away—a portrait of the old man's stern face hangs over the bar.

The Riverview

1101 Sophia Street, Fredericksburg, Virginia
540-373-6500

BUSINESS SEASON: all year
HOURS: open daily for lunch and dinner
WATERVIEW: Rappahannock River
CREDIT CARDS: AE, MC, Visa
HOUSE SPECIALTIES: oysters Riverview, spicy black bean cakes, crab stew, lobster
  bisque, pasta, lobster tail, crab cake, stuffed shrimp, crab imperial, catch of the day,
  tilapia, seafood sampler, Southside chicken grill, prime rib, filet mignon

George Washington knew Fredericksburg well from a boyhood spent playing in its streets, swimming in the Rappahannock River and perhaps cutting down a tree or two! Charles Weimer III played in the same streets and explored the bustling waterfront as Washington did, and in 1995 he built (actually *re*built from Arbuckles, opened in 1981) this riverbank restaurant which is known as one of the best in the state.

I'd recommend starting with Oysters Riverview—freshly shucked oysters layered with spinach, crumbled bacon, breadcrumbs and freshly grated Parmesan cheese, baked till bubbly and garnished with Hollandaise sauce. Follow it with a hearty crab stew and then the combination seafood sampler for an entrée. You'll enjoy a meaty crab cake, crab imperial, shrimp, scallops and a tilapia filet. Complement your meal with one of the 19 wonderful wines Charles has chosen. George would be proud of this place!

Kilmarnock Crab Dip

½ lb.   regular crab meat
8 oz.   cream cheese, softened
½ cup   sour cream
2 tbsp.   mayonnaise
1 tbsp.   lemon juice
1¼ tsp.   Worcestershire sauce
½ tsp.   dry mustard
           pinch garlic salt
1 tbsp.   milk
¼ cup   cheddar cheese, grated
           paprika for garnish

Remove cartilage from crab meat. In a large bowl, mix cream cheese, sour cream, mayonnaise, lemon juice, Worcestershire sauce, mustard, and garlic salt until smooth. Add enough milk to make mixture creamy. Stir in 2 tablespoons of the grated cheese. Fold crab meat into cream cheese mixture. Pour into greased 1-quart casserole. Top with remaining cheese and paprika. Bake at 325° until mixture is bubbly and browned on top, about 30 minutes. Serve with French bread chunks or crackers.

Great Wicomico Crab Dip

1 lb.   crab meat
16 oz.   cream cheese
6 tbsp.   white wine
2 tsp.   horseradish sauce
6 tbsp.   minced onion
2 tbsp.   milk
2 tsp.   Worcestershire sauce
           paprika

Soften cream cheese and mix with remaining ingredients. Place in pie plate or shallow casserole. Sprinkle with paprika and bake 15 minutes at 350° until bubbly. Serve with crackers or toast.

10: About the Virginia Shoreline of the Potomac River

Nestled between the Rappahannock and Potomac Rivers, the Northern Neck is a narrow, picturesque peninsula less than two hours away from the hustle and bustle of Washington, DC. The Potomac, with headwaters in the Allegheny Mountains and mouth on the Chesapeake Bay, flows along its northern shore, measuring 2 to 7 miles wide and navigable even for deep draft merchant ships all the way to Alexandria, Virginia.

Our culinary tour begins in tiny Kinsale, Virginia and covers the Virginia shoreline all the way to Alexandria. The listings in this chapter vary from open air cafés where you pick crabs on picnic tables, to elegant formal dining, but all provide outstanding cuisine, courteous service, and pleasant surroundings … and all have a grand view of the water..

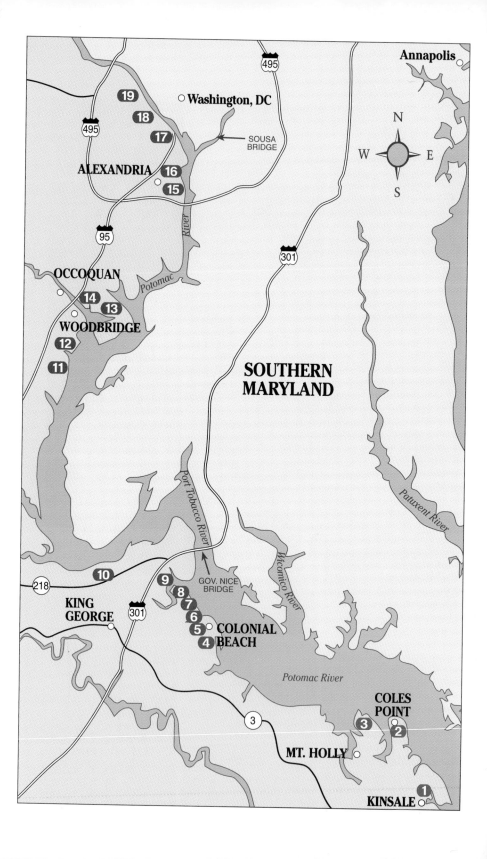

Potomac River Virginia Shoreline Waterside Dining

INCLUDES: Kinsale, Coles Point, Mt. Holly, Colonial Beach, King George, Dumfries, Woodbridge, Occoquan, and Alexandria, Virginia

1. The Mooring Restaurant
2. The Pilot's Wharf Restaurant
3. Mt. Holly Steamboat Inn
4. Dockside Restaurant
5. Parker's Crab Shore
6. Monroe Bay Landing Restaurant
7. Riverboat
8. The Happy Clam Seafood Restaurant
9. Wilkerson's Seafood Restaurant
10. Fairview Beach Crab House
11. Tim's Rivershore Restaurant & Crab House
12. Pilot House Restaurant
13. Geko's Waterfront Restaurant
14. Sea Sea and Co.
15. Cedar Knoll Inn
16. Dandy Cruise Ship
17. The Seaport Inn
18. The Chart House
19. Potowmack Landing

❶

The Mooring Restaurant
Route 608, Kinsale, Virginia
804-472-2971

BUSINESS SEASON: all year

HOURS: open Sunday, Monday and Thursday for dinner; Friday and Saturday for lunch and dinner; closed Tuesday and Wednesday

WATERVIEW: Yeocomico River

CREDIT CARDS: DC, MC, Visa

HOUSE SPECIALTIES: crab stuffed mushroom caps, Chesapeake seafood pie, baked stuffed shrimp, crispy fried oysters, prime rib, Virginia backfin crab cake dinner

The small town of Kinsale was named for Kinsale County, Cork, Ireland. In Gaelic, Kinsale means "head of the salt water." The Mooring Restaurant, located at the Yeocomico Marina on the West Yeocomico, is tucked around and inside of Horn Point.

The Mooring is a home converted into a restaurant. The original white shingled building with its beautiful climbing roses now has an addition: a large modern dining room with floor-to-ceiling windows. The menu is not large, but the food is good. Owner Garry Keckley recommended, the stuffed shrimp which I agree is the best thing on the menu. Another good choice is the Virginia backfin crab cake dinner. I also tried a daily special that was not on the menu, a truly outstanding seafood gumbo. The Mooring Restaurant is a delicious port of call!

The Pilot's Wharf Restaurant

Route 612, Coles Point, Virginia
804-472-4761

BUSINESS SEASON: seasonal

HOURS: open Wednesday through Monday for lunch and dinner; closed Tuesday

WATERVIEW: Potomac River

CREDIT CARDS: AE, MC, Visa

HOUSE SPECIALTIES: local rockfish, Norwegian salmon Dijon, chef's signature pasta, French lamb chops, Captain Peter's crab meat cocktail, seafood kabob, salmon cakes, cabbage and sausage soup

This "house of fish" serves some very good seafood specialties. Appetizers are superb, including Captain Peter's crab meat cocktail and the marinated herring with sour cream and onions, which is one of the best. The pasta dishes, especially the stuffed seashells in marinara sauce, are prepared with just the right amount of seasoning. Entrées include Norwegian Salmon Dijon: broiled salmon filled with onions and mushrooms in a rich cream sauce enhanced with dijon mustard. And don't miss the seafood kabob: skewered seafood and vegetables chargrilled and served on a bed of rice pilaf. Another favorite dish is the local rockfish filet fried, broiled, or sautéed and served with the chef's twin sauces. The atmosphere at the Pilot's Wharf is lively and the decor is nautical. Richmond Chef Robert Hayes has found a new home here in Bay Country.

Mt. Holly Steamboat Inn

Route 202, Mt. Holly, Virginia
804-472-3336

BUSINESS SEASON: seasonal
HOURS: open daily for dinner only
WATERVIEW: Nomini Creek/Potomac River
CREDIT CARDS: AE, DC, Disc, MC, Visa
HOUSE SPECIALTIES: local seafood dishes, soft-shell crabs, crab cakes, steaks, chicken,
    seafood platter, oysters and ham country style, crab Norfolk, stuffed shrimp, fried
    oysters, prime rib

Your hosts at Mt. Holly Steamboat Inn are Manfred and Margie Soeffing. Their menu
welcomes diners with the following story: In a bygone era, two blasts on the pilot-
house horn announced a riverboat's arrival. Exuberant passengers pressed along the
starboard rail as a deckhand lowered the gangway to a dock at a country inn. After a
long day of stops at tidewater ports along the Potomac, a cold drink awaited them
in the shade of towering trees. The setting was one of comfort and relaxation. As they
made their way to the three-story clapboard hotel, the passengers paused at a bluff
overlooking the water's edge to watch the sunset over Nomini Creek.

Today, the tradition continues. In the kitchen, the chef tosses soft-shell crabs into
a pan. On the lawn, the inn-keepers greet you with smiles, handshakes, and "Welcome
to The Steamboat Inn!"

④
Dockside Restaurant

Monroe Point, Colonial Beach, Virginia
804-224-8726

BUSINESS SEASON: all year

HOURS: open Saturday and Sunday for breakfast, lunch, and dinner; open Wednesday through Monday for lunch and dinner; closed Tuesday

WATERVIEW: Monroe Bay/Potomac River

CREDIT CARDS: AE, Disc, DC, MC, Visa

HOUSE SPECIALTIES: steamed crabs, oyster stew, steam bucket, crab cake and Virginia ham, fresh salmon, fried shrimp, black Angus New York strip, center cut pork chops

The Potomac River provides much of the fine seafood served at the Dockside Restaurant and Martin's Tavern. The Dockside staff take pride in catering to diners who are drawn to the tranquil bank of the Potomac and who are particular about their seafood. The chef personally selects the seafood and meats several times during the week and obtains the season's freshest crabs and oysters daily, and the jumbo lump crab meat is always hand picked.

Dockside's open air porch is an excellent place to feast on hot, steamed blue crabs, sip on a frosty glass of beer, and enjoy the panoramic view of the Potomac River. Martin's Tavern, a British-style pub, provides a cozy, intimate dining atmosphere. At either place, you'll enjoy fresh Potomac oysters on the half shell or summer-time cuisine with an imported ale or a perfectly blended mixed drink from the bar.

5

Parker's Crab Shore

1016 Monroe Bay Avenue, Colonial Beach, Virginia
804-224-7090

BUSINESS SEASON: April through October

HOURS: open daily for lunch and dinner

WATERVIEW: Monroe Bay

CREDIT CARDS: DC, Disc, MC, Visa

HOUSE SPECIALTIES: crab cakes, imperial crab, crab salad, crab Norfolk, soft crab, steamed shrimp, filet of fish, fried clams, fried oysters, steamed crabs, seafood platter, crab shore sampler

On the Potomac River, near the birthplaces of George Washington, Robert E. Lee and James Monroe, Colonial Beach prospered as farmland for the landed gentry during the 1700s. By the late 19th century, the lure of waterfront property started a building boom of large Victorian houses and quaint hotels which continued well after the town's 1892 incorporation. One of its most distinguished residents, Alexander Graham Bell, discovered, as did many others, that the "Beach" was a delightful summer retreat.

Something *you'll* discover when you visit is the down home goodness of Parker's Crab Shore. Along with the delicious steamed crabs, owners Bobby and Shirley Jenkins offer one of the best seafood platters anywhere. It includes fried shrimp, spiced shrimp, crab ball, fried scallops, fish fillet, shoestring clams and crab salad and is served with french fries and a trip to the salad bar. Sounds good, doesn't it?

Monroe Bay Landing Restaurant

11 Monroe Bay Avenue, Colonial Beach, Virginia
804-224-7360

BUSINESS SEASON: all year
HOURS: open daily for lunch and dinner
WATERVIEW: Monroe Bay
CREDIT CARDS: MC, Visa
HOUSE SPECIALTIES: crab cakes, catch of the day, fried shrimp, seafood platter, New
York strip, prime rib, honey-dipped fried chicken, oysters on a bun, steamed crabs,
filet of flounder, soft-shell crab sandwich

The early 20th century brought riverboats and tourists to Colonial Beach in large
numbers, when dance halls and legalized gambling made the town a favored weekend resort for the Washington area.

Colonial Beach also earned its name of "Oyster Capital of the Potomac," with many
skirmishes fought just offshore during the Oyster Wars. An annual event that always
brings folks back to "the beach" is the Potomac River Festival held in early June. The
town swells with more than 25,000 visitors which means you may have to wait a while
for a meal. But Monroe Bay Landing is woth the wait. The Landing Special features
mouthwatering filet of fresh fish broiled in a spicy hot lemon and butter sauce. If you're
a fried fish fan, try the Special. It's all you can eat with hush puppies and cole slaw.

Riverboat

301 Beach Terrace, Colonial Beach, Virginia
804-224-7055

BUSINESS SEASON: all year

HOURS: open daily for breakfast, lunch, and dinner

WATERVIEW: Potomac River

CREDIT CARDS: DC, Disc, MC, Visa

HOUSE SPECIALTIES: prime rib, crab dip, shrimp scampi, stuffed shrimp, crab cakes, crab Norfolk, baked stuffed flounder, steamed crabs, filet mignon, surf 'n' turf, crab salad, snockered shrimp

The address of the Riverboat on the Potomac is Colonial Beach, Virginia, but you'll actually be dining in Maryland. The prosperous restaurant and off-track betting parlor is built on pilings out over the Potomac River, and the Potomac River is within Maryland's jurisdiction. Hence the sign as you enter: "Welcome to Maryland." It is this unique location that allows the Riverboat to operate an off-track betting parlor (OTB for those in the know), because OTBs are legal in Maryland, but not in Virginia.

The Riverboat offers something for everyone. The Potomac Room has fine dining with a magnificent view of the river. Weather permitting you can sit on the Deck, where you can enjoy the best steamed crabs on the Beach. Or just view the river and beach while you have your favorite frozen drink. Come by car, raft, boat or jet ski.

The Happy Clam Seafood Restaurant

Route 205, Colonial Beach Avenue, Colonial Beach, Virginia
804-224-0248

BUSINESS SEASON: all year
HOURS: open daily for lunch and dinner
WATERVIEW: Potomac River
CREDIT CARDS: MC, Visa
HOUSE SPECIALTIES: broiled seafood kabobs, broiled flounder, fisherman's platter,
    steamed or spiced shrimp, southern fried chicken, Smithfield ham and crab quiche,
    fried clams, broiled combination Norfolk platter, German chocolate pie

Poised on a soaring bluff above the Potomac River, not far from Virginia's Popes Creek, is Stratford Hall, one of the great residential landmarks in American history. The visitor who enters the gate at Stratford is driving over the same road used by the family of patriots named Lee, two of whom grew up to be the only brothers to sign the Declaration of Independence. Four generations of Lees were born in a big upper-floor bedroom. A tiny net-draped cradle sits by the window, on the spot where it once rocked the infant Robert E. Lee, destined to head the Armies of the Confederacy. I am inspired by this history and also by the food at the nearby Happy Clam.

Take, for example, the Happy Clam's broiled imperial combo platter. It comes with large succulent shrimp stuffed with Chesapeake crab meat and two imperial crabs—plus a salad bar, hot hush puppies, french fries, or twice-baked potato.

⑨

Wilkerson's Seafood Restaurant

Route 205, Colonial Beach, Virginia
804-224-7117

BUSINESS SEASON: all year

HOURS: open daily for lunch and dinner

WATERVIEW: Potomac River

CREDIT CARDS: MC, Visa

HOUSE SPECIALTIES: steamed crabs, Potomac River rockfish, rockfish topped with crab
meat, backfin crab meat and shrimp casserole, imperial crab, fried oysters, backfin
crab meat cocktail, seafood combination platters

Seafood has been important to the commerce and pleasure of the people of Virginia
since colonial days. The history and reputation of Wilkerson's Restaurant is based upon
family traditions that have contributed to the State's reputation for fine seafood cuisine.

Wilkerson's was founded in May 1946 by Herbert Wilkerson and his son Walter.
From that first year through the early 1970s, Wilkerson's also served as a major whole-
saler and distributor of crab and oyster meats, supplying large grocery chains and other
restaurants throughout a multi-state area. The restaurant is still operated by the
Wilkerson family, and its reputation for quality has never been compromised. Give
Wilkerson's a visit and enjoy an outstanding seafood combination platter.

10
Fairview Beach Crab House

5435 Pavilion Drive, King George, Virginia
540-775-7500

BUSINESS SEASON: May 1 to late September

HOURS: open Tuesday through Friday for lunch only; Saturday and Sunday for lunch and dinner; closed Monday;

WATERVIEW: Potomac River

CREDIT CARDS: AE, DC, Disc, MC, Visa

HOUSE SPECIALTIES: fried catfish, stuffed flounder, pan sautéed crab cakes, steamed crabs, crab and shrimp salad combo, broiled scallops, crab Norfolk

Fairview Beach Crab House is a large, popular place situated along the banks of the Potomac River in an area that has seen many changes over the years. The restaurant is built on pilings and sits out over the water. The grounds once thrived as an amusement park with a waterslide and campground, and many of the old pavilions still stand but have seen better days.

There's nothing extraordinary here, just consistently good cuisine. The crabs are excellent, and I also suggest you give the crab Norfolk a try—it's jumbo lump crab meat broiled and topped with a wine butter sauce. This is a place where you can sit back and relax while you watch patrons pull up in their boats. On the day of my last visit, a dozen kids were swimming and playing in the water. It was fun to see, and 50 years ago, I'd have been in the water with them!

⑪
Tim's Rivershore Restaurant & Crab House

1510 Cherryhill, Dumfries, Virginia
703-441-1375

BUSINESS SEASON: all year
HOURS: open daily for lunch and dinner
WATERVIEW: Potomac River
CREDIT CARDS: AE, DC, Disc, MC, Visa
HOUSE SPECIALTIES: fried soft-shell crab dinner, steamed crabs, deviled crab dinner, broiled Rivershore platter, crab soup, clam chowder, cole slaw, baked beans, potato salad, t-bone steak

You won't find Tim's by accident, and you might be stopped at a railroad crossing to let a freight train by. Once across the tracks, follow them on a gravel road for a quarter mile, to a fun and funky little crab cookery—a true example of what "Bay Country" is all about.

The menu at Tim's Rivershore is a good introduction to Chesapeake seafood cooking, like crabs steamed in vinegar and beer and topped with salt and red pepper seasoning. For entrées, don't go home without sampling the Rivershore seafood platter: crab cake, fish filet, scallops, oysters, shrimp, and clams. The decor is indescribably bizarre and the open air deck attracts a young, lively clientele on the weekends. This spot is one of Susie's favorites, where a red VW delivery proclaims, "In claw we trust".

12

Pilot House Restaurant

16216 Neabsco Road, Woodbridge, Virginia
703-221-1010

BUSINESS SEASON: all year

HOURS: open for dinner only; closed Monday

WATERVIEW: Neabsco Creek/Potomac River

CREDIT CARDS: AE, CB, DC, Disc, MC, Visa

HOUSE SPECIALTIES: catch of the day, cold seafood combination platter, stuffed
butterfly shrimp, rainbow lake trout, filet of sole, lobster and backfin crab sautéed in
butter, crab cakes, ocean perch, stuffed soft-shell crabs

The Pilot House is one of those places that become old favorites right away because
the atmosphere is warm and comfortable, the food always good, and the service friendly.
Once a barge, the Pilot House was remodeled to look like a paddleboat, and the atmosphere is absorbing—you'll dine surrounded by a fascinating collection of nautical
antiques and collectibles. The upstairs lounge has a wonderful view of the river and
surrounding area—just the place for a nightcap after a perfect meal.

The Pilot House is known for its steaks. The New York strip sirloin, t-bone, and
filet mignon have a flavor that is distint but not overwhelming. The seafood, whether
soft crabs, crab cakes, filet of sole, or flounder stuffed with imperial crab, keeps people coming back. Plan to spend several hours when you visit here.

Geko's Waterfront Restaurant

13188 Marina Way, Woodbridge, Virginia
703-494-5000

BUSINESS SEASON: closed October to March
HOURS: open daily for lunch and dinner
WATERVIEW: Occoquan River
CREDIT CARDS: AE, DC, MC, Visa
HOUSE SPECIALTIES: Lonestar ribs, choice center cut New York strip, honey lime
   chicken breast, baby back ribs, backfin crab cakes, chilled oysters on the half shell,
   fresh broiled salmon, grilled swordfish steak Dijon

The deck of Geko's provides a view of a wide stretch of the Occoquan River where speedboats race to the Route 1 bridge and back again, cabin cruisers make way to the Potomac River toward the Chesapeake Bay, and sailboats meander and drift on a calm day. This sprawling restaurant has several very large dining rooms as well as a dance area with space for a large band, a raised porch, and, of course, the outdoor deck with its white tables and chairs and large umbrellas emblazoned with "Schweppes" logo.

The menu has changed toward the conservative since the early days when Southwestern cuisine was the mainstay. Featured now are fresh seafood, hearty beef and steak entrées, and an extended raw bar. Your host here is Chris Boos. Search him out. He's there to please you!

14

Sea Sea and Co.

201 Mill Street, Occoquan, Virginia
703-494-1365

BUSINESS SEASON: all year
HOURS: open daily for lunch and dinner
WATERVIEW: Occoquan River
CREDIT CARDS: AE, C, CB, DC, MC, Visa
HOUSE SPECIALTIES: oyster shooter, oysters on the half shell, grilled shrimp salad, steamer sampler, mariner's platter, shrimp and scallops pasta, rainbow trout almandine, stuffed flounder

The quaint artist community of Occoquan, Virginia, just minutes from I-95, is miles away from modern life in tempo and lifestyle. In 1734, it was the site of a public tobacco warehouse, but now its commerce is based on the artsy shops that line its narrow streets. At one end of Mill Street is a small museum if details on the town's history interest you. At the other end is Sea Sea and Co., in a well-designed building that has the appearance of an old sailmaker's shop.

A friendly stained glass sea horse on the front door sets the mood for what's inside. Large windows and high ceilings allow abundant light on the blue tablecloths, white chairs, red napkins, boating flags of all colors, ceiling fans and well-groomed plants. Outside is a deck open-air dining overlooking the picturesque river.

15

Cedar Knoll Inn

9030 Lucia Lane, Alexandria, Virginia
703-799-1501

BUSINESS SEASON: all year
HOURS: open Tuesday to Sunday for lunch and dinner; closed Monday
WATERVIEW: Potomac River
CREDIT CARDS: AE, DC, Disc, MC, Visa
HOUSE SPECIALTIES: onion soup gratinée, lobster bisque, trout supreme, lemon basil
linguine, roast duck, paella valenciana, baked seafood casserole, chicken Seville,
Caesar steak, authentic Spanish tapas

Mount Vernon, the treasured estate of George and Martha Washington is not only America's most popular historic home, it's also one of our country's oldest ongoing preservation projects. Washington's elegant mansion has been meticulously restored to its appearance in the last year of his life, from the paint colors on the walls to the actual arrangement of the furnishings, many of which are original. The ptoperty on which stands Cedar Knoll Inn was one owned by George Washington himself?

Located within a stone's throw of Mount Vernon, perched on the banks of the Potomac River, Cedar Knoll serves continental cuisine complemented by chef specialties that are distinctly Mediterranean in flavor. Specialties include paella valenciana, zarzuela de Mariscos, roast duck Seville, and authentic Spanish tapas.

16

Dandy Cruise Ship

Zero Prince Street, Alexandria, Virginia
703-683-6076

BUSINESS SEASON: all year
HOURS: open daily for lunch and dinner
WATERVIEW: Potomac River
CREDIT CARDS: AE, C, CB, DC, MC, Visa
HOUSE SPECIALTIES: prime rib, shrimp, fish of the day, cornish game hen, shrimp with
  crab meat stuffing, broiled salmon, poached salmon, chocolate mousse, deep dish
  apple pie

Leaving from its dock in historic Old Town Alexandria, the Dandy Restaurant Cruise
Ship will float you down the river on a Sunday afternoon. Or you can enjoy an evening
dining/dancing cruise while you view the lights of the Nation's Capital, the Jefferson
and Lincoln Memorials, Washington Monument, Kennedy Center, Watergate, Georgetown, exciting Washington Harbour, and Roosevelt Island.

Depending on the time of your visit, you can expect the chef to prepare some of
these "Dandy delights": Fresh spinach salad with fresh mushrooms, English walnuts,
and mandarin oranges; chicken marengo or a boneless breast of chicken in a lightly
seasoned Spanish sauce, served with fluffy rice. The fish dish may be flounder or haddock, always tender, flaky, and succulent, served with a delicate white wine sauce. It's
a "dandy way" to enjoy the Potomac River and all it has to offer.

The Seaport Inn

6 King Street, Alexandria, Virginia
703-549-2341

BUSINESS SEASON: all year
HOURS: open daily for lunch and dinner
WATERVIEW: Potomac River
CREDIT CARDS: AE, DC, MC, and VISA
HOUSE SPECIALTIES: Captain's platter (fried or broiled), surf 'n' turf, crab cakes, soft-shell crab platter, mahi mahi, whole fresh flounder, smoked trout salad, salmon steaks, New England lobster, tuna, swordfish, bouillabaisse

There's history everywhere in Old Town Alexandria. George Washington once walked these streets—surveyed them, actually—greeted his friends here, and attended Christ Church for services. George and his friend Colonel John Fitzgerald spent many pleasant times recalling military experiences and toasting business enterprises in the George Washington Tavern Room on the ground floor of the Seaport Inn. If only these walls could talk (walls, by the way, that are made of sand, water and oyster shell mortar and measure 28 inches thick), what stories they could tell! Upstairs a modern second floor dining room offers a panoramic view of the Potomac River.

Seaport Inn seafood specialties include crab imperial and crab and shrimp Norfolk (sautéed in a buttery wine sauce). Depending on availability, try the soft-shell crabs floured, dusted with salt and pepper, then sautéed in butter.

18

The Chart House

One Cameron Street, Alexandria, Virginia
703-684-5080

BUSINESS SEASON: all year
HOURS: open daily for dinner; open Sunday for brunch and dinner
WATERVIEW: Potomac River
CREDIT CARDS: AE, DC, Disc, MC, Visa
HOUSE SPECIALTIES: prime rib, steaks, seafood, baked rockfish with almond and citrus
crust, backfin lump crab cakes, Maine lobster, lobster bisque, oysters Rockefeller,
clams casino, New York strip, filet mignon

Captain's Row, near the Alexandria waterfront on Prince Street, is a block of quaint old row houses built in the manner of English seaport towns. Many were built by the seafaring sailing ship masters who made Alexandria their land home. Visitors can enjoy a walk down the cobblestone street or along the Cameron Street Promenade by the water. The Chart House Restaurant is between the old torpedo plant and the river's edge. It has been described as a "futuristic lighthouse" complete with two stately watchtowers.

Once inside the sprawling eatery, you can't help but notice the scenic view. In the middle of the room is a well-stocked salad bar. The entrées change frequently. One day's selection of fresh seafood may include baked scallops, mahi mahi, coconut chunky shrimp, Maryland crab cakes, Norwegian salmon, and grilled swordfish. The Chart House adds a nice touch to Old Town with its warmth and tropical splendor.

19

Potowmack Landing

Daingerfield Island, George Washington Memorial Parkway, Alexandria, Virginia
703-548-0001

BUSINESS SEASON: all year

HOURS: open daily for lunch and dinner

WATERVIEW: Potomac River

CREDIT CARDS: AE, DC, MC, Visa

HOUSE SPECIALTIES: live Maine lobster, fresh catch of the day, black Angus
   porterhouse, chicken and dumplings, fresh grilled vegetables, grilled Tuscan
   plank steak, chicken and dumplings, Mrs. Daingerfield's lasagna

The Port of Alexandria lured shipwrights and sea captains with its deep water harbors and abundance of raw materials. One was mariner Bathurst Daingerfield, father
of John B. Daingerfield, after whom this island was named. Many changes have taken
place since those days. For one, the Potowmack Landing Restaurant has been recently
remodeled and presents a new menu. There are several dining areas, three outdoor decks,
plenty of glass, and a super view of the Nations Capital.

   My favorite dish here is Captain John's creative catch. Each day Chef Marcel Langlais
features several fish which may be grilled, blackened, broiled, or sautéed as you please.
The many sauces available include fisherman's tartar sauce, cherry jalapeño glaze, roasted
green chile-yogurt sauce, herbed aioli, orange-chipotle sauce, and roasted red pepper sauce.

Rivershore Crab Quiche

1	partially baked 9-inch pastry shell
1 lb.	crab meat
2 tbsp.	finely chopped shallots
2 tbsp.	butter
2 tbsp.	finely chopped parsley
1 tsp.	finely chopped tarragon
2 tbsp.	wine
4	eggs
1½ cups	heavy cream
	salt and pepper
¼ cup	grated Parmesan cheese

Simmer the chopped shallots in the butter for just a few minutes, until they are soft, but not brown, put crab meat in a mixing bowl, keeping pieces as large as possible; add shallots, parsley, tarragon, and wine. In a separate bowl, beat together the eggs and cream, then gently fold into the crab meat mixture. Season with salt and pepper. Pour into the pastry shell, sprinkle with Parmesan cheese, and bake in 350°F oven until custard is set about 30 minutes. Serve hot. Serves: Four.

Rivershore Crab au Gratin

1 lb.	crab meat
2 tbsp.	butter, melted
	salt and pepper to taste
½ cup	cream or evaporated milk
2	egg yolks, well beaten
½ cup	grated cheese

Combine butter, crab meat, salt and pepper; cook for 5 minutes without browning. Mix cream with egg yolks; add to hot crab meat mixture. Cook for 4 minutes over low heat, stirring constantly. Pour into large casserole; sprinkle cheese over top. Bake in 350°F oven until cheese is melted. Serves: Four.

11: About the Maryland, Washington, DC Shoreline of the Potomac River

A close look at a detailed map reveals that along the 100 miles of shoreline from Washington, DC to Point Lookout in Southern Maryland, nearly 30 rivers or creeks feed into the Potomac, making the area a natural for waterside dining. We begin our culinary adventures at the Washington Harbor just below the fall line in northwest Washington, DC. We continue downriver, through the southwest waterfront, where a cluster of restaurants provides a variety of cuisine. Still further downriver, Popes Creek, Maryland offers three crab houses within walking distance of each other. Crabs are layered in a pot of vinegar and water, covered with a mixture of salt, pepper, ginger, mustard and the chef's secret ingredients, and steamed just long enough for the shells to turn an appetizing bright red. It can't be beat—and it's all with a view of the water.

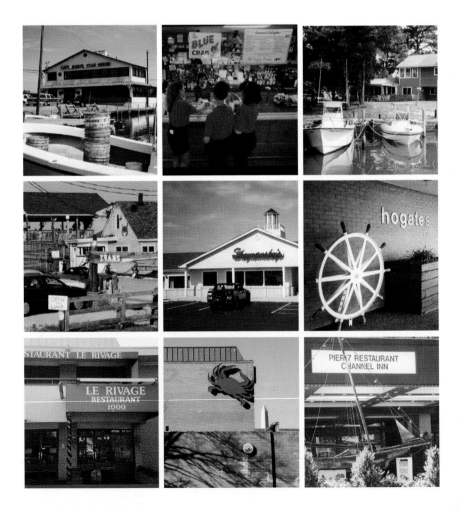

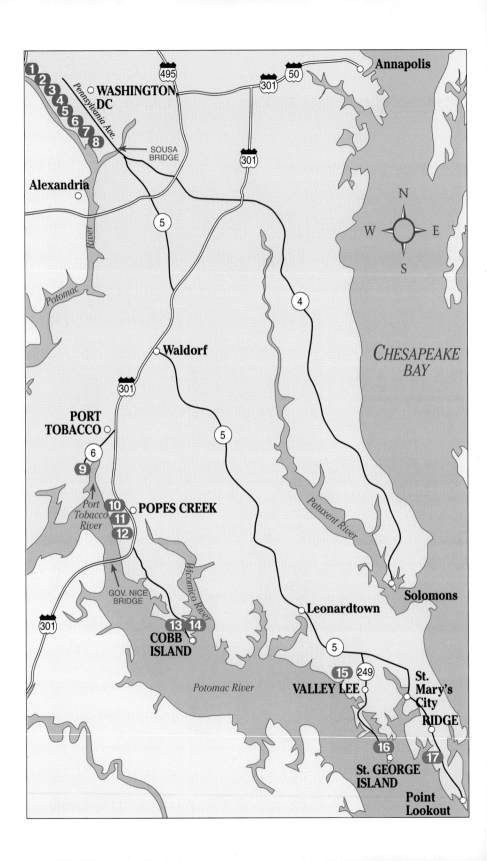

Potomac River
Washington, DC, Maryland Shoreline
Waterside Dining

INCLUDES: Washington, DC; Popes Creek, Cobb Island, Port Tobacco, Valley Lee, St. George Island, and Ridge, Maryland

1. Riverside Grille
2. Tony and Joe's Seafood Place
3. Sequoia
4. Le Rivage
5. Phillips Flagship
6. Hogates Seafood Restaurant
7. Pier 7 Restaurant
8. Odyssey III Cruise Ship
9. Port Tobacco Turf Club
10. Robertson's Crab House
11. Captain Billy's Crab House
12. Pier III Seafood House
13. Captain John's Crab House
14. Shymansky's Restaurant
15. Cedar Cove
16. Evans Seafood
17. Scheible's Crab Pot Restaurant

❶
Riverside Grille

3050 K Street, NW., Washington, DC
202-342-3535

BUSINESS SEASON: all year

HOURS: open daily for lunch and dinner

WATERVIEW: Potomac River

CREDIT CARDS: AE, DC, Disc, MC, Visa

HOUSE SPECIALTIES: steak and pasta, grilled pepper scallops, sautéed jumbo shrimp, chicken piccata, broiled filet of salmon, cheese stuffed tortellini, linguini with clams, Potomac porterhouse

Georgetown was incorporated in 1789, and the State of Maryland recognized it as a major tobacco port in 1751. Back then the harbor was filled with square-rigged sailing ships, and schooners waited for loads of Maryland tobacco. Georgetown has evolved into an area with expensive homes, trendy shopping during the day, and chaotic bar scenes at night. Park your car or tie your boat up at the Washington Harbor and have a tasty lunch or dinner at the Riverside Grille.

A sure bet on the menu is the Riverboat Gambler—jumbo shrimp sautéed with red and green peppers in a sweet Sambuca sauce. (Sambuca is an Italian aniseed-flavored liqueur.) Grilled pepper scallops is another house specialty—fresh jumbo Atlantic scallops topped with roasted peppers and served with penne, marinara sauce, and fresh vegetables. The "Riverside Grille" provides the perfect background for a festive dinner.

②
Tony and Joe's Seafood Place

3000 K Street, NW., Washington, DC
202-944-4545

BUSINESS SEASON: all year
HOURS: open daily for lunch and dinner
WATERVIEW: Potomac River
CREDIT CARDS: AE, DC, MC, Visa
HOUSE SPECIALTIES: barbecued scallops, oysters on the half shell, hot crab dip,
   Maryland crab soup, cream of crab soup, seafood stew, tuna steak, mahi mahi,
   halibut, swordfish, red snapper, grouper, salmon, dover sole

The Potomac River boldly flows nearly 400 miles from West Virginia's Alleghenies
to Point Lookout on Chesapeake Bay—the fourth largest watershed on the East Coast.
George Washington recommended building the nation's capital on its banks. Today,
on a Georgetown River bank at Washington Harbor sits Tony and Joe's Seafood Place,
where the view over the lighted fountains to the river beyond is entrancing any time
of day.

Select from appetizers like barbecued scallops wrapped in bacon, freshly shucked
Pine Island oysters on the half shell, or hot crab dip. I tried two of the four soups,
and both were delicious—the Maryland crab and the cream of crab. For dinner, try
the seafood stew, an extravaganza of mussels, clams, shrimp, scallops, and fish gently
simmered in a saffron seasoned tomato broth. Service is friendly and efficient.

❸

Sequoia
3000 K Street, NW., Washington, DC
202-944-4200

BUSINESS SEASON: all year
HOURS: open daily for lunch and dinner
WATERVIEW: Potomac River
CREDIT CARDS: AE, DC, Disc, MC, Visa
HOUSE SPECIALTIES: Sequoia clams casino, Caesar salad, peppered shrimp linguine,
Japanese hibachi-style grilled salmon, swordfish chop, cioppino, pan-roasted prime
filet mignon

The Sequoia attracts the rich and famous, conventioneers, boaters, and tourists from around the world. There's a touch of gilded elegance in the air: polished cherrywood floors, a sweeping, multi-level dining room, panoramic views, and a five-level garden with more than a thousand flowering and evergreen plants. Here you can enjoy lunch, brunch, dinner, or cocktails along with the breezes of the Potomac River.

The cooking style is regional American with emphasis on pleasant peppery Southwest, Jamaican, and Italian favorites. Maryland Low Country seafood bisque is a good way to begin. Follow that with "cioppino," a San Francisco style fisherman's stew with pan-roasted lobster, shrimp, mussels, clams, scallops, and calamari in a spicy broth of tomato, olives, potatoes, and saffron. The menu is particularly appropriate to the international mix of the clientele. All is beautifully prepared and served.

④
Le Rivage

1000 Water Street, SW., Washington, DC
202-488-8111

BUSINESS SEASON: all year

HOURS: open Monday through Friday for lunch and dinner; Saturday and Sunday for dinner only

WATERVIEW: Washington Channel/Potomac River

CREDIT CARDS: AE, DC, Disc, MC, Visa

HOUSE SPECIALTIES: crab meat sautéed with butter, sautéed flounder, fresh lobster (steamed, roasted or grilled), beef stew with fresh vegetables, pepper stea

L e Rivage is a special place to take that special person. It's spacious and confortable and if you can secure a window table, you'll be able to carry on an intimate conversation. Or do as I do and sit outside on the large deck overlooking the water, the boat dock and the municipal fish wharf and seafood market.

Le Rivage specializes in French food served in an elegant atmosphere. Entées include *coquille St. Jacques au buerre de noisette* (scallops baked with hazelnut butter), *cassolette de crabe Norfolk* (fresh crab meat sautéed with butter, lemon and Virginia ham), and *sauté de boeuf aux petits legumes* (beef stew with fresh vegetables). I think the most interesting items on the menu are found in the daily special section—that's where you'll find unique creations such as rockfish and salmon sautéed with artichokes and cream sauce, or grilled halibut with salmon caviar beurre blanc.

⑤

Phillips Flagship

900 Water Street, SW., Washington, DC
202-488-8515

BUSINESS SEASON: all year

HOURS: open daily for lunch and dinner

WATERVIEW: Washington Channel/Potomac River

CREDIT CARDS: AE, DC, Disc, MC, Visa

HOUSE SPECIALTIES: waterman's harvest buffet, crab legs and shrimp, crab combo, whole Maine lobster, grilled fish of the day, roast beef and mashed potatoes, rotisserie chicken, crab cakes, steamed crabs

My earliest memories of Phillips go back to the late fifties in Ocean City, Maryland. When Shirley and Brice Phillips opened their small carryout "crab shack," it was an ideal outlet to sell surplus crabs and crab meat from the family's seafood packing plant on Hooper's Island in the Chesapeake Bay. Their second season they expanded, and over the years the business has grown tremendously. In December 1985, the Phillips family opened Phillips Flagship in our Nation's capital. Phillips Flagship has a scenic view of the Washington Channel and is close to many Washington landmarks.

You'll dine inside among lush greenery and stained glass or outside on the patio overlooking boat slips and the city's skyline. Fresh seafood, daily menu specials, and a lively piano bar are all a part of what keeps me coming back after all these years. Once you visit Phillips, you'll be back.

Hogates Seafood Restaurant

800 Water Street, SW., Washington, DC
202-484-6301

BUSINESS SEASON: all year
HOURS: open daily for lunch and dinner
WATERVIEW: Washington Channel/Potomac River
CREDIT CARDS: C, CB, DC, Disc, MC, Visa
HOUSE SPECIALTIES: New England clambake, Hogates original 1938 mariner's platter,
Norfolk shellfish sampler, broiled captain's platter, original rum buns, pot of
steamed mussels, chargrilled jumbo shrimp

Hogate's spectacular seafood restaurant has been a Washington tradition for over
55 years. It began as a small seafood stand in Ocean City, New Jersey, in 1928 and
moved to Washington, DC in 1938. In 1972, the Washington waterfront area under-
went a complete redevelopment program and Hogate's moved from across the street
on Maine Avenue to its present location overlooking the Potomac River.

I still remember my first taste of the house specialty, the incredible "Rum Bun," in
the early 1960s. On my most recent visit, I didn't have to ask—soon after I was seated,
a giant "Rum Bun" was placed in front of me. I chose the 30-item buffet and feasted
on New England clam chowder, seafood Newburg, beef stew, fresh baked bluefish, and
a fresh garden salad. I didn't even look at the dessert bar, but I wrapped the remains
of my Rum Bun, placed it in my camera bag, and carried it home to enjoy later.

Pier 7 Restaurant

650 Water Street, SW., Washington, DC
202-554-2500

BUSINESS SEASON: all year

HOURS: open Monday through Friday for, lunch and dinner; Saturday and Sunday for dinner only

WATERVIEW: Washington Channel/Potomac River

CREDIT CARDS: DC, MC, Visa

HOUSE SPECIALTIES: crab imperial, prime rib, baked stuffed flounder, crab cakes, roast duck, bouillabaisse à la Marseillaise, fresh daily specials

There's a spectacular view of East Potomac Park from the picture windows of this elegantly appointed restaurant in one of the country's outstanding small hotels. For an elegant, gourmet meal, step into Pier 7, where the interior will remind you of a cruise ship: crisp white linen, mahogany woodwork, and impeccable service. The Engine Room lounge features live jazz music four nights a week, and weather permitting, you can have your cocktail on the terrace and enjoy the marina surroundings.

On a recent visit, I chose the soup du jour—a beef barley—and followed it with a Pier 7 crab sandwich. The lump crab meat with herbs and a delicate seafood seasoning was stuffed into fresh baked French bread and topped with cheese sauce. On another visit, I tried the antipasto with fresh mozzarella cheese, sliced garden tomato, grilled vegetables, and highlighted with fresh pressed olive oil. All delicious!

Odyssey III

600 Water Street, SW., Washington, DC
202-488-6000

BUSINESS SEASON: all year, weather permitting

HOURS: open daily for lunch and dinner

WATERVIEW: Potomac River

CREDIT CARDS: AE, DC, Disc, MC, Visa

HOUSE SPECIALTIES: buffet selections, herb roasted chicken, grilled filet of beef tenderloin, roasted salmon, scallop salad, chargrilled filet mignon, penne pasta, plenty of fresh fruit

When you call to make a reservation on the Odyssey III, you'll be asked to confirm with a major credit card—and there are no refunds. You'll set sail for a three-hour dinner cruise or a two-hour lunch cruise that's spectacular in any season. In spring, you'll enjoy the District's most exquisite view of the cherry blossoms. In summer, the warm breezes and sunsets are unsurpassed. In autumn, the city's luminescent glow offers some of the most colorful vistas of the year, and in winter, when wind and tide conditions prevent navigation to Kennedy Center and Georgetown, an alternate route is taken. Designed specifically to travel beneath the capital's historic bridges, Odyssey is the only vessel of its kind in the United States. From striking glass atrium dining rooms, you'll enjoy a seasonal menu prepared fresh on board daily. Be swept away by the vibrant pulse of live music, or simply stroll the decks as you cruise the scenic Potomac shores.

⑨
Port Tobacco Turf Club
7536 Shirley Boulevard, Port Tobacco, Maryland
301-932-0063

BUSINESS SEASON: all year
HOURS: open Tuesday through Sunday for lunch and dinner; closed Monday
WATERVIEW: Port Tobacco River
CREDIT CARDS: MC, Visa
HOUSE SPECIALTIES: Caesar salad, southern Maryland crab cakes, lemon chicken, chicken marsala, filet mignon, fettucini alfredo, grilled swordfish, filet mignon, porterhouse steak, pasta primavera

In 1608, when Captain John Smith sailed up the Potomac River, he made a map of the Indian Village of Potopaco. Around 1638, Father Andrew White, a Jesuit missionary, converted the Queen of the Potopaco Indians and her subjects to Christianity and composed a grammar and dictionary in the Indian language.

At the Port Tobacco Turf Club, the only language you'll need is race track lingo. Phrases like, "Starting gate," "Down the back stretch," and "Turning for home" fill the air. This restaurant is officially an off-track betting site, so you won't have to venture to the tracks to make your wagers. Fifty televisions around the restaurant will help you keep track of the action. Toward the rear of the building is the most elite section, where you can enjoy a fine dinner in a subdued setting where you can check on your bets between bites.

10

Robertson's Crab House

Popes Creek Road, Newburg, Maryland
301-934-9236

BUSINESS SEASON: Memorial Day through Labor Day; closed January and February; open weekends only in March and April

HOURS: open daily from 11 AM to 9 PM

WATERVIEW: Potomac River

CREDIT CARDS: MC, Visa

HOUSE SPECIALTIES: steamed crabs, spiced shrimp, crab cakes, boiled and fried dinners, home fried chicken, oyster platter, crab imperial platter

On Maryland Route 301 South, look for a large billboard pointing the way to Robertson's Crab House; its the first restaurant about 3 miles down Popes Creek Road. By water the address is Popes Creek, Maryland. To travelers arriving by land or sea, the white building with blue trim proudly announces, "Seafood–Steaks–Spirits."

Behind the bar you'll find Joe Robertson, with his warm, friendly smile. Who knows, but always asks "Good evening, Whitey. Would you like a menu or are you having crabs?" Knotty-pine paneling evokes memories of the late 1950s. Brown butcher paper, vinegar bottles, pleated paper cups, mallets and paring knives are set ceremoniously for a crab-picking celebration. On each and every visit, Joe has always been behind the bar and the crabs have been delightful.

Photograph by Noel Schwab

11

Captain Billy's Crab House

Popes Creek Road, Popes Creek, Maryland
301-932-4323

BUSINESS SEASON: March to December

HOURS: open daily for lunch and dinner

WATERVIEW: Potomac River

CREDIT CARDS: MC, Visa

HOUSE SPECIALTIES: steamed crabs, crab cake platter, prime rib, whole steamed Maine lobster, key lime pie, the backfin, a special house drink, catch of the day stuffed with crab imperial, fresh seafood platters, crab meat in garlic butter

Back in the days of mail boats and locomotives, when electricity was new to Popes Creek and work was just beginning on the Potomac River Bridge, nine-year-old Billy Robertson sold his first crabs on this very shore. With a little luck and a lot of determination, Captain Billy has made his crab house what it is today. Billy and co-owner Celene Graves are still adding on to suit their customers' needs, but there are some things that time can't change, and one is the feeling you get when you go to a Southern Maryland crab house like this one. Some foods need their natural environment in order to develop every nuance of their flavor, and Maryland blue crabs need rock salt, peppery bay seasoning, tangy vinegar, and smooth melted butter. It's all here, and it includes a full view of the Maryland and Virginia shorelines.

Photograph by Noel Schwab

12

Pier III Seafood House

Popes Creek Road, Newburg, Maryland
301-259-4514

BUSINESS SEASON: all year
HOURS: open Tuesday through Sunday for dinner; Thursday through Sunday for lunch
and dinner; closed Mondays
WATERVIEW: Potomac River
CREDIT CARDS: MC, Visa
HOUSE SPECIALTIES: steamed crabs, steaks, steamed spice crab soup, clam chowder,
oyster stew, the Admiral's seafood platter, crab imperial, soft-shell crabs

When I asked owner Tom Jenkins what made Pier III different from the rest, he replied,
"We're the third crab house on the right. We have to be different." I found the food
excellent and the staff young and friendly, paying meticulous attention to every detail
that makes a guest comfortable, including giving tours about the property. I timed my
latest visit on the day school had let out in the area, and the restaurant was filled with
teachers celebrating with a traditional Southern Maryland crab feast.

I remember this restaurant from years ago, and it's improved since then. It's no
longer dark and dingy, but open and airy. Walls have been torn down, a new bar and
crab eating room have been added, and palm trees add to the decor. Outside there's
now a waterside bar, a bandstand, and a pro-size volleyball court. I know you'll be
pleasantly surprised with both the service and the food.

Captain John's Crab House

16215 Cobb Island Road, Newburg, Maryland
301-259-2315

BUSINESS SEASON: all year

HOURS: open daily for breakfast, lunch, and dinner

WATERVIEW: Neale Sound/Potomac River

CREDIT CARDS: MC, Visa

HOUSE SPECIALTIES: steamed crabs, imperial crab, broiled sea trout, jumbo stuffed shrimp, oyster basket, Captain John's platter, crab lover's platter, island platter, crab cakes, fried oysters, fresh fish, bean soup

Since this crab house opened in the early 1960s, I've returned time and again, and I've enjoyed every meal, from locally caught crabs to Captain John's famous bean soup. Captain John's is operated by Jack and Christine Yates and their son, Skip, who has taken on much of the day-to-day operation. Christine works with the waitresses, and Jack oversees the crab cooking operation, a skill he has perfected over the years.

The menu is mostly seafood, but chicken and steaks make a token appearance. The imperial shrimp—five broiled jumbo shrimp—are topped with imperial crab and provolone cheese; and the succulent, fresh oysters are accompanied by your choice of any two side dishes and hot rolls with butter. John's unique wooden-box crab steamer, tempting desserts, such as carrot cake and strawberry cloud cake, and a house specialty drink, the Sea Nettle Sting make this restaurant a special place.

14

Shymansky's Restaurant

Cobb Island Road, Newburg, Maryland
301-259-2881

BUSINESS SEASON: all year

HOURS: open daily for breakfast, lunch, and dinner

WATERVIEW: Neale Sound/Potomac River

CREDIT CARDS: MC, Visa

HOUSE SPECIALTIES: steamed crabs, prime rib, cream of crab soup, mariner's platter, frog leg dinner, deviled crab, fried chicken, lobster Norfolk style, broiled flounder, stuffed shrimp

Shymansky's Restaurant and Marina is adjacent to Captain John's Crab House at the foot of the Cobb Island Bridge. Cobb Island was not always an island—it was once connected to the mainland by a sand bar that was dry at extreme low tide, when it was possible to drive a buggy or walk across. But thanks to storms, floods, and the Corps of Engineers, which began to dredge Neale Sound in the 1930s, it's now really an island. Cobb Island's claim to historical fame is that here in 1900, Reginald Fessenden and Frank Very first sent intelligible speech by wireless telephony!

Today history is being made in the kitchen at Shymansky's Restaurant as Butch and Pat Shymansky oversee the delightful mariner's platter, the house specialty for over 50 years. It includes scallops, fried fish, crab cake, shrimp, oysters, or soft crab, depending on the season, and comes with salad bar and vegetable, rolls and butter.

15

Cedar Cove

Route 249, Valley Lee, Maryland
301-994-1155

BUSINESS SEASON: seasonal

HOURS: open daily for lunch and dinner

WATERVIEW: Herring Creek/Potomac River

CREDIT CARDS: AE, Disc, MC, Visa

HOUSE SPECIALTIES: homemade chili, clam chowder, tuna salad, ribeye steak
  sandwich, crab cakes, crab melt, fried shrimp platter, grilled chicken breast platter,
  ribeye platter

Adjacent to Cedar Cove Marina in Valley Lee, Maryland, Cedar Cove caters to boaters, truckers, tourists, local business people, families, and those in the know, and has done so for many years. Cedar Cove is one of those places that become old favorites very fast because the atmosphere is warm and comfortable, the food always good, and the service always friendly. It serves American food with some nice little touches.

It's known for the crab cake platter: freshly picked crab meat hand-patted, pan-fried, and served with a delightful cocktail sauce. Platters come with potato salad or cole slaw, chips and grilled bread. Several other platters offered are the rib eye, fried shrimp, and grilled chicken breast, and Cedar Cove also offers french fries with a rich gravy—not heart-healthy, perhaps, but hard for me to pass up. Cedar Cove is not fancy but it's fun, and I always stop here when I'm in this neck of the woods.

Evans Seafood

Route 249, St. George Island, Maryland
301-994-2299

BUSINESS SEASON: all year

HOURS: open Tuesday through Friday for dinner only; Saturday and Sunday for lunch
and dinner; closed Mondays, winter hours may change

WATERVIEW: Potomac River and St. George's Creek/St. Mary's River

CREDIT CARDS: MC, Visa

HOUSE SPECIALTIES: crab imperial, soft-shell crab (a real delight), deep fried oysters,
crab cakes, steamed crabs, combo platters, broiled rockfish

St. George was the patron saint of England, and this island in the Potomac River,
it is believed, was named for him. Another possibility is that the name came from St.
George's River, now called St. Mary's River. An indisputable fact is that Evans Seafood
is one of the most popular restaurants in the state. It's in the middle of the tiny pine-
dotted island and is owned by Ronnie and Carol Evans, who have recently made remark-
able changes. For one, the entrance to the restaurant is now through what was once
the cabin of a Bay-built workboat. They also built the Island Breeze Crab Deck on
top of the old oyster house and it offers wonderful views of both the Potomac River
and St. George's Creek.

One thing they did *not* change was the wonderful way they prepare steamed crabs.
Tell Carol, Whitey sent ya.

17

Scheible's Crab Pot Restaurant

23 Wynne Road, Ridge, Maryland
301-872-5185

BUSINESS SEASON: May through October

HOURS: open daily for breakfast, lunch, and dinner

WATERVIEW: Potomac River

CREDIT CARDS: MC, Visa

HOUSE SPECIALTIES: fresh fish, crab soup, crab cakes, soft-shell crabs, oysters any
style, crabbettes, day's catch, broiled shrimp, captain's platter, and Friday and
Saturday seafood combo

The first settlers to this part of Maryland arrived in the *Ark and Dove* on the 25th
of March, 1634. The land they purchased from the Indians included the Village of
Yaocomico, which they renamed St. Maries. Today's attractions include a replica of
the square-rigged *Maryland Ark and Dove* and Point Lookout State Park, where the
Department of Natural Resources has built a 600-foot concrete pier. If you're here
for some angling, head for Scheible's Fishing Center, the "Bluefish Capital of the World"
and home to some of the best fishing on the Chesapeake Bay.

If you're here to eat, Scheible's Crab Pot is my choice. And if you visit on a Friday
or Saturday, try the seafood combo. It features crabbettes (spicy bite-size crab cakes
you eat like popcorn), steamed or fried shrimp, and fried or broiled fish. It's "all you
can eat" from 5 PM to 8 PM. Its humble exterior conceals a vaiety of seafood delights.

Evans Seafood Broiled Rockfish

Spread fish filet on a piece of foil on a baking sheet. Squeeze a fresh lemon onto fish, then sprinkle a bit of garlic powder and salt on fish. We also put melted butter and some finely-ground cracker crumbs on top, then broil until fish begins to flake and separate. The cooking time varies according to thickness of the filet. If you have a large piece of fish, then you should place fish further from broiler to give more time for the fish to cook through.

St. George's Broiled Shrimp

2	pounds raw, peeled, deveined shrimp
3	cloves garlic, minced
½ cup	melted butter
2 Tbs.	lime juice
½ tsp.	salt
	freshly ground pepper
	chopped parsley

Cook garlic in butter until tender. Remove from heat. Add lime juice, salt and pepper. Arrange shrimp in a single layer on a baking pan, 15" x 10" x 1". Pour sauce over shrimp. Broil about 4" from source of heat for 8 to 10 minutes or until shrimp are pink and tender. Sprinkle with parsley. Serves: Six.

Evans Seafood.

12: About the Patuxent River Area

The most visited town along the Patuxent River (named after the Patuxent Indians, who built more than 20 towns along the shore) is Solomons Island, home of the Calvert Marine Museum. The museum's exhibits include the *Wm. B. Tennison*, the oldest passenger-carrying vessel on the Bay, and the Drum Point lighthouse, commissioned in 1883, which sat at the mouth of the Patuxent until it was moved in 1975 and painstakingly restored. Also of interest is the J.C. Lore Oysterhouse, owned by the Museum. The Oysterhouse exhibit depicts the seafood harvesting and processing business that once flourished in Solomons.

Experience the spirit of Solomons as you enjoy a bowl of oyster stew in one of the many fine restaurants described in this chapter. Or try a crab cake at any one of these establishments—they're all very tasty, and they all come with a view of the river.

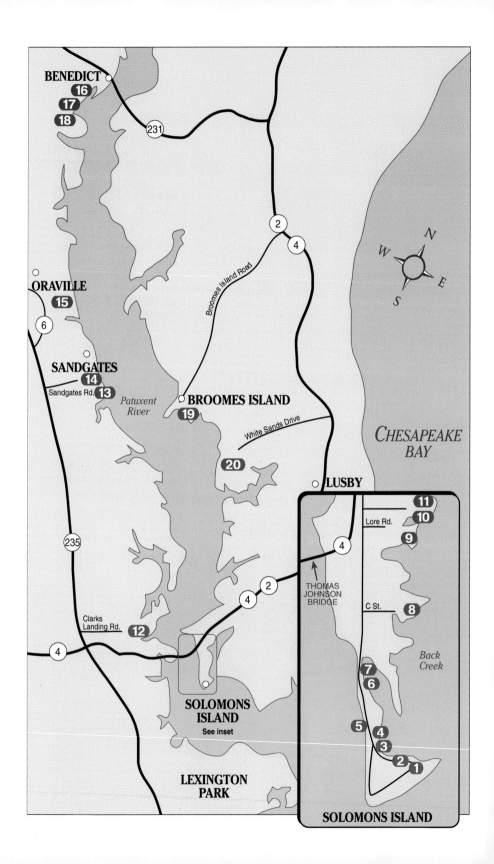

Patuxent River Waterside Dining

INCLUDES: Solomons Island, Hollywood, Mechanicsville, Oraville, Benedict, Broomes Island, and Lusby, Maryland.

1. Harbor Island
2. China Harbor
3. Lighthouse Inn
4. Bowen's Inn
5. Solomon's Pier Restaurant
6. Rhumb Line Inn
7. Catamarans Restaurant
8. The Dry Dock
9. The Captain's Table
10. The Naughty Gull
11. The Maryland Way Restaurant
12. Clarke's Landing Restaurant
13. Seabreeze Restaurant & Crab House
14. Sandgates Inn
15. The Drift Inn
16. Chappelear's Place
17. Tony's Riverhouse
18. Ray's Piers Restaurant
19. Stoney's Seafood House
20. Vera's White Sands

Harbor Island

120 Charles Street, Solomons Island, Maryland
410-326-9522

BUSINESS SEASON: all year
HOURS: open Monday through Thursday for dinner only; Friday through Sunday for
lunch and dinner
WATERVIEW: Back Creek/Patuxent River
Credit Cards: DC, Disc, MC, Visa
HOUSE SPECIALTIES: sautéed shrimp, scallops, crab meat, clams and artichoke hearts,
broiled flounder, stuffed grape leaves, gyro platter, veal parmigiana, surf & turf

Solomons Island is at the extreme tip of the peninsula that is Calvert County, named
for Maryland's founding family of 1634. Solomons was identified as Bourne's Island
in 1680 and by 1740 it was called Somervell's Island. In 1867 it became known as
Solomon's Island courtesy of the oyster packing plant established by Isaac Solomon.
Today Solomons is the home of the Calvert Marine Museum and the Drum Point
Lighthouse … and Harbor Island Restaurant.

Harbor Island is known for its island favorites like fresh seafood Norfolk—jumbo
shrimp, sea scallops and lump crab meat baked in a casserole with chablis wine, a
touch of garlic, lemon juice, and butter. Or how about broiled flounder topped with
sautéed shrimp, clams and mushrooms and a touch of garlic, shallots, and white wine?
It's served with a baked potato and salad, and it's good!

2

China Harbor

77 Charles Street, Solomons Island, Maryland
410-326-6888

BUSINESS SEASON: all year
HOURS: open daily for lunch and dinner; closed Mondays during winter season
WATERVIEW: Back Creek/ Patuxent River
CREDIT CARDS: AE, DC, Disc, MC, Visa
HOUSE SPECIALTIES: seafood soup, moo goo gai pan, chicken with garlic sauce, shrimp
   tempura, broccoli in oyster sauce, vegetarian delight, honey garlic chicken, sesame
   beet, Hong Kong shrimp, shrimp with walnuts

Yvonne Lee, owner of China Harbor, offers an odyssey of authentic Chinese cuisine
especially chosen to please the palate. My selection of moo goo gai pan arrived with
a heaping bowl of steamed rice. The platter was joyful and alive with color—green
peas, orange carrots, water chestnuts, mushrooms, Chinese cabbage, and a perfect
sauce—all enhancing the white meat chicken. When I asked Lee the secret, she replied,
"It's my chef Yow Yow. Few chefs have his talents. He specializes in all types of foods
from the many provinces of China. As for myself, I come from Hong Kong and my
dream has always been to design and own a restaurant. That dream has been fulfilled."

You'll fulfill *your* dream of eating the best Chinese food you've ever tasted when
you dine at China Harbor.

③
Lighthouse Inn
1463 Solomons Island Rd., Solomons, Maryland
410-326-2444

BUSINESS SEASON: all year
HOURS: open daily for dinner
WATERVIEW: Back Creek/Patuxent River
CREDIT CARDS: AE, DC, Disc, MC, Visa
HOUSE SPECIALTIES: grilled herb chicken, filet and crab combination, filet mignon, surf and turf, stuffed mushrooms, clams casino, fresh catch of the day, baked stuffed shrimp, crab cakes, crab imperial, soft-shell crabs, mariner's platter

Your first impression of the Lighthouse Inn is its spaciousness. A two-story wall of glass overlooks a wide deck that offers summertime patrons a chance to enjoy warm gentle breezes from Back Creek. Whether you sit upstairs or downstairs in the main dining room, you'll have an enchanting view. In the Skipjack Bar, a replica of a Chesapeake Bay work boat, the crew serves a creditable Bloody Mary from the transom.

The menu offers a creative variety of traditional seafood dishes. One of my all-time favorites is the baked stuffed shrimp. Large shrimp are butterflied, stuffed with *crabulos* crab imperial. And don't go home without trying the succulent soft-shell crabs—a Southern Maryland favorite—pan-sautéed until golden brown. Remember, good food takes time to prepare, so relax with a cocktail or share a bottle of wine with friends while you await a delicious meal.

④
Bowen's Inn

14630 Solomon's Island Road, Solomons, Maryland
410-326-6790

BUSINESS SEASON: all year
HOURS: open daily for lunch and dinner
WATERVIEW: Back Creek/Patuxent River
CREDIT CARDS: MC, Visa
HOUSE SPECIALTIES: Bowen's crab imperial, fisherman's seafood platter, Maryland crab
cake platter, Maryland fried chicken, spaghetti and meatballs, prime rib, scallop
casserole, Back Creek shrimp, New York strip

Bowen's Inn is a hotel, restaurant and bar known all along the East Coast. It's been
in the same family since 1918. The bar was built around 1928 as a hotel annex, and
as business grew, so did the bar. In fact, parts of the Inn are still being renovated. In
1990 a deck was enclosed to make the new dining room and a new deck was added
to allow for outdoor dining (weather permitting). A new addition is the "Anticipation
II"—a modern 80-foot cruise ship that departs from the Bowen's dock.

So many choices! It's all up to you. Take a cruise or eat in the new dining room.
Bowen's crab imperial will please any appetite. The recipe has been used for over 50
years and you can have it with or without the meringue topping! If you come for the
prime rib, please note that it's only served on Friday and Saturday nights. The all-
crab-meat crab cakes can be had any time and can be ordered fried or broiled.

Solomons Pier Restaurant

14575 Solomons Island Road, Solomons Island, Maryland
410-326-2424

BUSINESS SEASON: all year

HOURS: open daily for lunch and dinner

WATERVIEW: Patuxent River

CREDIT CARDS: AE, Disc, MC, Visa

HOUSE SPECIALTIES: smothered chicken, surf & turf, steamed shrimp, steamed clams, fried oyster dinner, fried fisherman's platter, jumbo steak for two, stuffed flounder, scallops of the day, broiled platter

The Patuxent River was named after the Patuxent Indians encountered on its banks by English settlers. From its source at Parr's Ridge up near Frederick, Maryland, the peaceful, majestic Patuxent River flows through 110 miles of Maryland's diverse landscape. Where the river joins the Chesapeake Bay, its basin forms one of the most beautiful natural harbors in the world.

Solomons Pier's building was constructed in 1919 and in the early 1920s a waterslide was built from the top of the building so that people could descend in small boats and splash into the Patuxent River! That's all changed now—the only splash you may encounter is that of a wind surfer as you look out to enjoy the sunset. Try the fried oyster dinner—plump oysters, deep-fried to perfection and served with cocktail sauce, baked potato and vegetable of the day.

6

Rhumb Line Inn

14442 Solomons Island Road, Solomons Island, Maryland
410-326-3261

BUSINESS SEASON: all year
HOURS: open daily for lunch and dinner
WATERVIEW: Back Creek/Patuxent River
CREDIT CARDS: AE, MC, VISA
HOUSE SPECIALTIES: vegetarian pasta, steak Neptune, spicy pecan-crusted chicken,
   Rhumb Line platter, New York strip, crab strudel, island crab dip, tuna steak, stuffed
   shrimp, London broil, seafood primavera

The Rhumb Line Inn is in the heart of a fascinating natural history area. In nearby
Lusby is Calvert County's Calvert Cliffs State Park. The majestic Calvert Cliffs have
towered over the Chesapeake Bay for 15 million years. You can reach the cliffs by
hiking through this 1600-acre wooded park where more than 600 species of fossils
have been found.

After your hike, make a beeline for the Rhumb Line Inn. Don't miss the Rhumb
Line's signature dish, crab strudel—crab meat tossed with special spices, boursin cheese
and cognac, rolled in filo dough and broiled golden brown. The crab soup is also good—
hearty and chock full of fresh crab. It's pure flavor. Another wonderful dish is the spicy
pecan-crusted chicken—a tender chicken breast rolled in a pecan crust and served
with creole mustard cream sauce. Enjoy!

Catamarans Restaurant

14470 Solomons Island Road, Solomons Island, Maryland
410-326-8399

BUSINESS SEASON: all year

HOURS: open daily for lunch and dinner

WATERVIEW: Back Creek/Patuxent River

CREDIT CARDS: AE, DC, Disc, Visa

HOUSE SPECIALTIES: baby back ribs, half smoked chicken, prime rib, stuffed shrimp, soft-shell platter, rockfish filet, crab cake, stuffed shrimp, catch of the day, and from the steamer—clams, oysters, crab legs, and shrimp.

From the White House to the lighthouse: As you leave Washington, follow Pennsylvania Avenue through historic Southern Maryland. In a short time you'll be surrounded by historic homes and churches, fascinating museums, and beautiful parks. Within a short walking distance of the Drum Point Lighthouse (located at the Calvert Marine Museum), you'll find some splendid eating places.

Catamarans Seafood, Ribs and BBQ, and Cabaña Bar Restaurant is the first restaurant on the left as you enter Solomons Island. Here you'll enjoy crab puffs (crab balls dipped in beer batter and stuffed with a spicy cheese sauce), a selection of delicious soups, and many entrées. You'll be pleased with the Catamarans special (black Angus sirloin basted in Montreal seasoning and grilled to your liking), or the catch of the day (your choice of fish prepared blackened, broiled, Cajun or grilled).

⑧
The Dry Dock

245 C Street, Solomons, Maryland
410-326-4817

BUSINESS SEASON: all year
HOURS: open daily for lunch and dinner; closed Tuesdays during winter season
WATERVIEW: Back Creek/Patuxent River
CREDIT CARDS: AE, MC, Visa
HOUSE SPECIALTIES: grilled salmon, beef tournedos, crab soup and cakes, catch of the
day, prime rib au jus, surf & turf, grilled beef tenderloin, grilled rockfish, jumbo
shrimp scampi, lemon peppered lamb chops

The beautiful Bay offers something for all moods, from Baltimore's historic downtown districts to the harborplace markets of Annapolis. But if you'd like to see how
a yachting center handles the needs of today—complete with a 30-ton train lift and
a 60-ton railway—head for Solomons Island. The best way to view the workings of
this busy waterfront business is from the Dry Dock, located in the boatyard of Zahniser's
yachting center.

My latest visit was rewarded by the Dry Dock's incredible flounder and crab florentine—fresh flounder poached in white wine, wrapped around spinach, stuffed with crab,
topped with hollandaise sauce, and served over rice. The Dry Dock has it all—fine food,
fine drink and a spectacular view. Because the Dry Dock is very popular, the management suggests that you make a reservation if you plan to visit on the weekend.

9

The Captain's Table

875 Lore Road, Solomons Island, Maryland
410-326-2772

BUSINESS SEASON: all year
HOURS: open daily for breakfast, lunch, and dinner
WATERVIEW: Back Creek/Patuxent River
CREDIT CARDS: DC, Disc, MC, Visa
HOUSE SPECIALTIES: chicken breast marsala, roast turkey and dressing, seafood au gratin, orange roughy parmesan, prime rib of beef, Maryland crab cakes, crab imperial, baked orange pork chop

Fishing and oystering were prosperous businesses around Solomons Island in the early 1880s, when the fleet exceeded 500 vessels. The "Bugeye," enabled the oysterman to harvest his catch sunup to sundown in the shallow waters around Solomons. In the late 1800s the "patent tongs," invented by local blacksmith Charles Marsh, increased the oysterman's efficiency and became the primary method of shallow-water oyster gathering. I still go to the Captain's Table when the urge for oysters strikes. Nothing satisfies like a piping hot bowl of oyster stew.

An entrée lists one dozen fried oysters, golden brown (available in "R" months only). Another features surf and turf—a 6-ounce filet mignon and a 6-ounce lobster tail; or surf and surf—two 6-ounce lobster tails. I say, "Who needs the beef?" I'm happy with the seafood!

⑩
The Naughty Gull

499 Lore Street, Solomons, Maryland
410-326-4855

BUSINESS SEASON: all year
HOURS: open daily for lunch and dinner
WATERVIEW: Back Creek/Patuxent River
CREDIT CARDS: MC, Visa
HOUSE SPECIALTIES: baked chicken, seafood platter, crab cakes, rainbow trout, stuffed shrimp, New York strip and 5 ounces of scallops, porterhouse steak, half chicken, fried shrimp

Today's visitors to Solomons Island will not have the Drum Point Lighthouse to guide them into this quaint waterman's town. It once stood at the entrance to the Patuxent River where the river joins the Chesapeake Bay but now is at the Calvert Marine Museum. A short distance away is the Spring Cove Marina, where you'll find the Naughty Gull Pub Restaurant. Situated on a secluded cove, shaded by mature pine trees in a resort-like atmosphere, it provides generous southern Maryland cooking.

New owner Pat Emmons says, "Our unique setting features lively lounging and generous portions of homestyle meals. We make every effort to prepare each of our dishes to order." On my most recent visit, the specials were crab cakes and a soft-shell crab sandwich. *I* wanted a crab cake with a soft-shell sautéed on the side. No problem! Everything I tasted was expertly prepared, distinctively seasoned, and delicious.

The Maryland Way Restaurant

155 Holiday Drive, Solomons Island, Maryland
410-326-6311

BUSINESS SEASON: all year
HOURS: open daily for breakfast, lunch, and dinner
WATERVIEW: Back Creek/Patuxent River
CREDIT CARDS: AE, CB, DC, Disc, MC, Visa
HOUSE SPECIALTIES: fish du jour, broiled salmon steak, baked flounder with oyster
   stuffing, seafood Norfolk, seafood pasta primavera, broiled seafood platter,
   Maryland Way crab cake platter

The 170-room Solomons Holiday Inn Hotel is designed around a large courtyard which opens to the water, allowing you to enjoy dockside activities. The Hotel lets you select your mood—you can sip Margaritas at the dockside "Sandbar" while you enjoy lively evening entertainment or take a leisurely stroll outdoors and watch the lights reflecting on the water while listening to the rhythmic clank of halyards. The Maryland Way Restaurant and Lounge, also with a view of the water, offer excellent gourmet delicacies served in a relaxing yet elegant atmosphere.

For starters, why not try baked stuffed shrimp with crab imperial followed with a fresh garden salad. Now you're ready for an entrée. You can't go wrong ordering baked flounder with oyster stuffing. It comes with a choice of fettuccine, rice, or baked potato and is served with freshly baked corn fritters, banana bread and rolls.

⑫
Clarke's Landing Restaurant

Clark's Landing Road, Hollywood, Maryland
301-373-8468

BUSINESS SEASON: all year
HOURS: open daily for lunch and dinner
WATERVIEW: Mill Creek/Patuxent River
CREDIT CARDS: MC, Visa
HOUSE SPECIALTIES: world-class crab cake, steamed crabs, shrimp and chicken salads, crab muffin, filet of perch, Mill Creek seafood chowder, waterman's oyster stew, Maryland crab soup, burgers, Philly-style steak and cheese

After a five-year tour of the culinary Chesapeake, I thought I knew all the crab houses until I heard of Clarke's Landing in St. Mary's County. The restaurant, whose mainstay is fresh seasonal seafood, is on Mill Creek, about five miles upstream from Solomons Island. Owner Martha Keefe, who took over about three years ago, remodeled immediately, and you'll find fresh paint and new furnishings throughout.

Are you an oyster fan? Martha only buys the largest and plumpest Wicomico River oysters and fries them in her secret batter. Martha's World Class Crab Cake lives up to its name—Martha only uses the freshest, highest quality jumbo lump crab meat, tenderly blends it with a Smith Island-style spice mix, real mayonnaise, farm fresh eggs, and deep fries the mixture to a golden hue. And when it comes time for steamed crabs at Clarke's Landing, expect some of the best you have ever eaten.

(13)

Seabreeze Restaurant & Crab House

Sandgates Road, Mechanicsville, Maryland
301-373-5217

BUSINESS SEASON: all year
HOURS: open daily for lunch and dinner
WATERVIEW: Patuxent River
CREDIT CARDS: MC, Visa
HOUSE SPECIALTIES: queen steak dinner, king steak dinner, stuffed flounder, crab
cakes, steamed crabs, seafood platter, surf & turf, pizza, corn fritters, cream of crab
soup, oyster stew

The Seabreeze Restaurant and Crab House is one of a kind—the type of restaurant that could only exist in Bay Country. This local watering hole, pool room, crab house, and tiki bar has been around since southern Maryland's gambling days—when slot machines were so plentiful they outnumbered those in Las Vegas by three to one. Those days are gone now and the blaze of neon has dimmed. About the only things that remain are the hardwood floors.

Some folks come to the Seabreeze just to see Elvis (he's been seen here twice), but I come for the steamed crabs prepared with Bootie's Special Spice. Visit and enjoy the food, the fun, the tiki bar and the long fishing and crabbing pier that extends out into the Patuxent River. And who knows—maybe you'll see Elvis. (I think I caught a glimpse of a guy with long sideburns last time I was there!)

(14)
Sandgates Inn

Sandgates Road, Mechanicsville, Maryland
301-373-5100

BUSINESS SEASON: all year
HOURS: open daily for lunch and dinner
WATERVIEW: Patuxent River
CREDIT CARDS: AE, Disc, MC, Visa
HOUSE SPECIALTIES: crab soup, soft-shell crabs, crab cakes, steamed crabs, fried
   oysters, oyster stew, oysters on the half shell, steamed oysters, seafood chowder,
   stuffed shrimp, seafood platter

I've never been disappointed here with the service or the food at Sandgate Inn. In 1938 a private home was converted into a restaurant, and it has grown ever since. First, an outdoor deck was enclosed to make two large dining rooms. Recent exterior work includes a large carved crab on top and an outside deck, giving the opportunity to enjoy steamed crabs with the gentle breezes of the Patuxent River chasing away any insect intruders. Inside, owners Sissy and David Buckler have decorated with ship models, a U.S. flag and a crab flag.

The menu is limited—only 18 items, and four of them are oysters, including fried, steamed, on the half shell, and in a stew. There are also four ways to sample crabs: crab soup, soft-shell crabs, crab cakes, and steamed crabs—by the dozen.

15
The Drift Inn

Drift Inn Road, Oraville, Maryland
301-884-3470

BUSINESS SEASON: May to November
HOURS: open Friday for dinner only; Saturday and Sunday for lunch and dinner
WATERVIEW: Horselanding Creek/Patuxent River
CREDIT CARDS: none
HOUSE SPECIALTIES: steamed crabs, oysters, steamed shrimp, soft-shell crabs, crab
sandwiches, hamburgers

If Leonard Copsey had been here steaming crabs back in 1812, the British would never have marched to Washington, DC to burn the Capitol—they'd still be here feasting! But unfortunately, Leonard didn't open the Drift Inn until 1953. Some things have changed since that time (for example, back then, crabs sold for 50 cents a dozen), but one thing never will—the hours: the Drift Inn opens *only* on weekends. Leonard says, "That's how it started and that's how it'll be."

The Inn serves crab cakes, soft-shell crab sandwiches, and oysters in season. Leonard also offers hamburgers, but how anyone could choose a hamburger after seeing the crabs is beyond me. If you visit the Drift Inn today, you won't find anything fancy, but you will see a 400-foot pier that's open for boaters, and you'll meet Leonard's wife Josephine and other family members who make the Drift Inn "*the* place for crabs."

Chappelear's Place

Patuxent Avenue, Benedict, Maryland
301-274-9828

BUSINESS SEASON: all year

HOURS: open daily for lunch and dinner

WATERVIEW: Patuxent River

CREDIT CARDS: none

HOUSE SPECIALTIES: hamburger steak with fried onions, seafood platter, oyster stew (in season), homemade bean soup, crab cakes, fish sandwiches, soft-shell crab sandwiches, Maryland style crab soup

Benedict always brings back fond memories of my childhood. My father, Pop Schmidt, would arrive home from a day of fishing on the Patuxent River carrying a basket of large, fresh croaker, and in no time at all, Mom would have them frying in a cast-iron skillet. Even at that young age, names like Solomons, Patuxent, Point Lookout, and Benedict left permanent memories of pleasant family outings. Today when I visit here, my first stop is always Chappelear's Place. The rear porch of this tiny restaurant sits out over the water, and that's where I like to be. It reminds me of my Mom's kitchen, and like Mom's where there was always a pot of crab soup simmering away on the back burner of the stove.

The menu is limited, but crab cakes, crab soup, fresh sea trout sandwiches and oysters on the half shell or steamed or in a stew is a great way to begin.

17

Tony's Riverhouse

Patuxent Avenue, Benedict, Maryland
301-274-4440

BUSINESS SEASON: all year

HOURS: open daily for lunch and dinner

WATERVIEW: Patuxent River

CREDIT CARDS: MC, Visa

HOUSE SPECIALTIES: marinated swordfish, steamed crabs, crab cakes, grilled pork
   chops, lamb chops, New York strip, filet mignon, pork tenderloin, crab imperial,
   cream of crab soup, oyster stew

Time moves at a different pace in Benedict. The largest number of people who ever visited Benedict at one time was during the War of 1812, when 5,000 British invaded on the way to Washington, DC. Today, it's a great town to explore on foot with a camera or sketch pad.

Tony's sits on a spot of land that was once a stop for the steamboat lines that connected the many Chesapeake Bay towns. Established in1930 as Shorter's Place, the restaurant was operated by the same family until recently, when it was bought by Tony Arnold, who has given the place a new look. I noticed the building had a fresh coat of paint when I pulled up, and the old entryway has been redone. Inside, more tables have been added and forest green paint complements the knotty pine paneling. Whatever you do, don't pass up Tony's world-class crab cake. It's marvelous.

18

Ray's Pier Restaurant
DeSoto Place, Benedict, Maryland
301-274-3733

BUSINESS SEASON: all year

HOURS: open daily for lunch and dinner

WATERVIEW: Patuxent River

CREDIT CARDS: none

HOUSE SPECIALTIES: shrimp salad, crab cakes, steak and seafood gumbo, seafood
platter, soft crab sandwich, oyster stew, chili, clam chowder, bread pudding, filet
mignon, delmonico, liver and onions

"Downhome, genuine, and hearty" best describes the food served at Ray's Pier in
downtown Benedict, Maryland. People coming to Ray's for the first time all seem to
say, "I've been to Benedict 100 times and I never knew you were here." But once they
find Ray's, located at the end of DeSoto Place just at the foot of the Patuxent River
Bridge, they always return. Ray's Pier is owned by Ray and Pat Rawlings, whose pride
in their restaurant shows. Ray tends the long, friendly bar and greets customers with
a warm smile. Pat, who preps all the meals, says "I'm not a chef, but I love to cook."
Ray's Pier isn't fine, formal dining, but it *is* good food and there's plenty of it.

Specialties at Ray's Pier include oysters, soft-shell crabs (in season) and delicious
crab cakes. Let's not forget the homemade bread pudding and the extra special—everybody's favorite—shrimp salad.

Stoney's Seafood House

Oyster house Road, Broomes Island, Maryland
410-586-1888

BUSINESS SEASON: all year
HOURS: open daily for lunch and dinner
WATERVIEW: Island Creek/Patuxent River
CREDIT CARDS: MC, Visa
HOUSE SPECIALTIES: steamed crabs, crab cake, steamed shrimp, Broomes Island crab soup, seafood chowder, Stoney's steamer, fish sandwich (fresh-caught filet), snow crab legs, steamed mussels, crab claws, homemade potato salad, Stoney's super burger

I heard it was delicious, but when I took my first bite … WOW! Delicious and more. Stoney's crab cake sandwich is one of the best you'll ever try. Phil Stone says he opened Stoney's about eight years ago because "There was no crab house on this side of the Patuxent River in Calvert County." Today, Stoney's backfin crab cake sandwich brings enthusiastic raves from all parts of Bay Country and his steamed crabs are getting smashing reviews as well.

To get a taste of all sorts of steamed seafood, try the sizzling steamer. It includes Phil's special handpicked selection of fresh caught crustaceans piled high on a platter—and it's enough for two or more. You'll be delighted with the succulent crab legs, shrimp, lobster tails, mussels, crayfish and clams or oysters. Add a little garlic butter and you're set!

⑳
Vera's White Sands

1200 White Sands Drive, Lusby, Maryland
410-586-1182

BUSINESS SEASON: May to December
HOURS: open Tuesday through Saturday for dinner only; Sunday for lunch and dinner
WATERVIEW: St. Leonard's Creek/Patuxent River
CREDIT CARDS: MC, Visa
HOUSE SPECIALTIES: Mary's Maryland fried chicken, crab imperial, shrimp scampi, catch of the day, manicotti, seafood buerre blanc, crab cakes, rack of lamb, grilled scallops, lobster with crab imperial, osso buco

Vera's White Sands Restaurant & Marina is located on historic St. Leonard's Creek, approximately 2½ miles upstream at the entrance to John's Creek, off the Patuxent River. The Creek is wide and channel depth is 14 feet. St. Leonard's Creek is where Commodore Joshua Barney fought the British before their troops burned the Capitol in Washington.

The restaurant is the brainchild of owner Vera Freeman, a graciously articulate lady whose platinum shoulder-length hair and red and white pleated muumuu grace her surroundings. Dining rooms, corridors, and cozy corners of the restaurant are adorned with objects of art, oddities, and artifacts of Vera's world travels.

Cuisine is seafood, chicken, and steak, but don't be surprised to find a rack of lamb, osso buco, or manicotti with Italian sausage. Vera's White Sands is truly unique.

Chesapeake Bay Sampler Recipes

Solomons Island Crab Imperial

3	eggs
4 tbsp.	mayonnaise
2 tbsp.	dry white wine
2 tbsp.	sweet pickle relish
1 tsp.	dill weed
2 tsp.	seafood seasoning
1 lb.	lump backfin crab meat

In a bowl, whip the eggs until fluffy. Beat in the mayonnaise and wine. Add the pickle relish, dill weed and seafood seasoning and mix well. Gently fold in the crab meat, then spoon the mixture into buttered individual dishes. Bake at 375°F for 20 to 25 minutes or until lightly golden on top. Serves: Four.

Sautéed Flounder

1 tbsp.	oil
1 tbsp.	butter
1 lb.	flounder
1 tbsp.	lemon juice
1 tbsp.	chopped parsley

Sauté flounder in oil and butter for 10 minutes per inch of thickness measured at the thickest part of the fish, turning once halfway through cooking time. Remove to warm platter. Mix lemon juice and parsley with pan juices and pour over fish. Serves: Four.

Back Bay Shrimp Creole

2 lbs.	unpeeled raw shrimp
1	medium onion, chopped
1	small green pepper, chopped
½ cup	sliced celery
½ cup	salad oil
2 tbsp.	all-purpose flour
16 oz.	can tomatoes
6 oz.	can tomato sauce
2	garlic cloves, chopped
1	bay leaf
1 tsp.	salt
21 tsp.	chili powder
4	dashes hot sauce
1 cup	tomato juice
1 can	green peas
	hot cooked rice

Drop shrimp into boiling water to cover; simmer covered for 2 to 5 minutes; drain. Peel and devein shrimp; set aside. Sauté onion, garlic, green pepper, and celery in hot oil; add flour, and stir until smooth. Add tomatoes, tomato sauce, and seasonings; simmer 15 minutes. Add shrimp and tomato juice; cover and simmer 30 minutes. Add peas to shrimp mixture and cook an additional 10 minutes Serve over hot cooked rice. Serves: Six.

Surfside 7 Clams Casino

Casino Butter:
1 lb.	butter
¼ cup	minced garlic
¼ cup	minced red peppers
¼ cup	minced green peppers

Combine all ingredients. Add 1 teaspoon of casino butter to each clam on the half shell and top with 1¼" of raw bacon. Bake at 350°F until bacon is done, top with provolone cheese, melt. Serve with lemon wedge.

Baked Fish

1 lb.	fish filets, ¾ to 1½" thick, cut into serving size pieces
2 tbsp.	cornmeal
2 tbsp.	flour
¼ tsp.	paprika
	salt and pepper
1 tbsp.	oil
1 tbsp.	grated parmesan cheese

Pat fish dry with paper towels. Combine cornmeal, flour, paprika and dash each of salt and pepper in flat dish. Place oil in baking dish; heat in 425°F oven 1 minute. Dredge fish in cornmeal mixture; shake off excess. Place in baking dish and turn to coat with oil. Arrange fish pieces 1" apart. Sprinkle with parmesan cheese. Bake at 425°F allowing 10 minutes per inch thickness measured at its thickest part. Fish flakes when tested with a fork. Serve with your choice of sauce. Serves: Four.

Oysters on the Half Shell

36   oysters
        ice
        cocktail sauce
        lemon
        saltines

Wash oysters and chill thoroughly. Open and serve on cracked ice with cocktail sauce and saltines. Use lemon for garnish. Serves: Six.

Oysters Rockefeller

48   oysters on half shell
1 bnch.   spinach
2 bnchs. green onions
1   stalk celery
1 bnch.   parsley
1 stick   butter, melted
1½ cups bread crumbs
3 tbsp.   Worcestershire sauce
1 tbsp.   anchovy paste
            salt to taste
            hot sauce to taste
2 ozs.   Pernod
¾ cup   bread crumbs

Grind spinach, onion, celery and parsley very fine. Mix in 1 stick butter, melted and 1½ cups bread crumbs. Season with Worcestershire sauce, anchovy paste, salt and hot sauce to taste. Add Pernod and mix well. Put oysters in shells which are on rock salt, and cover each with some sauce. Cover with bread crumbs. Bake in 450°F oven until brown. Serve hot. Serves: Four.

Vic's Italia Pearls On the Beach

1 cup	pine nuts, toasted
3	eggs
3 cups	ricotta
1½ cups	grated parmesan cheese
½ tbsp.	hot pepper flakes
1 tsp.	white pepper
1 tsp.	oregano
1 tsp.	basil
3 tbsp.	parsley
½ tsp.	salt
1	handful shredded mozzarella cheese
12 oz.	jumbo pasta shells, cooked and drained

Mix all ingredients together. Stuff inside cooked pasta shells, roll in flour, dip in beaten egg wash and dredge in Italian bread crumbs. Deep fry at 350°F until golden and filling is hot (about 4 minutes). Serve with Marinara sauce. Serves: Four.

Vic's Italia By the Bay

Cambridge Crab Cocktail

1 lb.	crab meat
	lettuce
	cocktail sauce
	parsley
	lemon wedges

Remove any shell or cartilage from crab meat, being careful not to break the meat into small pieces. Arrange lettuce in 6 cocktail glasses. Place crab meat on top; cover with cocktail sauce. Garnish with parsley and lemon wedges. Serves: Six.

Patuxent River Fried Soft-Shell Crabs

12   cleaned soft crabs
          salt and pepper
          flour
          butter and oil for frying

Dry crabs with paper towel. Sprinkle with salt and pepper. Lightly coat with flour. Cook crabs in fry pan, in just enough oil and butter mixture to prevent sticking, until browned; about 5 minutes on each side.
Serves: Six.

Crab Meat Norfolk

2 tbsp.   butter
          juice of half lemon
1 lb.   crab meat
          salt and pepper to taste
          paprika
2 tbsp.   minced parsley
4 slices buttered toast

Heat the butter and juice of half a lemon in skillet. Add the crab meat, salt and pepper. Shake skillet to mingle flavors. When mixture is hot, dust with paprika and garnish with parsley. Serve on slices of buttered toast. Serves: Four.

Herrington's Pasta St. Croix

8	sea scallops
8	large shrimp, peeled
10	littleneck clams
1 lb.	cooked penne pasta
6	plum tomatoes, roughly chopped
1 tsp.	crushed garlic
10	large leaves of fresh basil
1 tbsp.	fresh oregano leaves
¼ cup	extra virgin olive oil
1 tbsp.	butter
	salt and freshly cracked black pepper

Marinate tomatoes:

Combine the tomatoes, garlic, basil, oregano olive oil and pepper. This mixture will turn out best when made at least 3 hours ahead of time.

Put the dish together:

Heat up 1 to 2 tablespoons of olive oil in a shallow sauté pan. When this is very hot, add your clams, shrimp and scallops. Sauté this for about 1 minute. Add your marinated tomatoes and cover the pan for 2 to 3 minutes to allow the clams to steam. Add the cooked pasta and mix so that the pasta heats up. Add the butter and mix well. Taste and season with salt if necessary. Serves: Two.

Herrington on the Bay Restaurant

Kent Island Oyster Fritters

1 pt.	shucked oysters
½ cup	evaporated milk
1 cup	pancake mix
2 tbsp.	cornmeal
1 tsp.	salt
¼ tsp.	pepper
¾ cup	peanut oil

Drain oysters, reserving liquor. Put oysters in bowl; mix in milk. Add pancake mix, cornmeal, salt and pepper. Mix well. (Batter will be thick.) Heat oil in fry pan. Drop batter into hot oil by tablespoons full making sure to include 2 oysters in each portion. Cook until brown on one side, 1 to 2 minutes. Turn carefully and brown the other side. Makes about 18 fritters.

NOTE: If batter becomes too thick on standing, thin with oyster liquor. Serves: Six.

Crisfield Sautéed Sea Trout

1 lb.	fish filets, ½ inch thick
	salt and pepper
	flour
1 tbsp.	butter
1 tbsp.	olive oil
	chopped parsley or dill
	lemon wedges for garnish

Pat fish dry with paper towels. Season lightly with salt and pepper. Coat fish with flour; shake off excess. In wide skillet, heat butter and oil on medium-high heat until it foams. Add fish. Cook until lightly browned, about 2 minutes. Turn carefully and brown second side. Fish is cooked when it begins to flake when tested with a fork at its thickest point. Transfer to heated platter. Sprinkle with parsley or dill and serve immediately. Serve with lemon wedges. Serves: Four.

Smithfield Cream of Crab Soup

1 lb.	lump crab meat
1 pt.	milk
1 pt.	cream
½ stick	butter
2 tbsp.	sherry
½ tsp.	ground mace
2 pcs.	lemon peel
¼ cup	cracker crumbs
	salt and pepper to taste

Put milk in top of double boiler with mace and lemon peel and allow to simmer for a few minutes. Then add crab, butter and cream and cook for 15 minutes. Thicken with cracker crumbs. Season with salt and pepper. Just before serving, add sherry. Serves: Six.

Southern Maryland Crab Soup

1 lb.	crab meat
1	large can tomatoes
6	potatoes, diced
2	medium onions, diced
2 cups	whole kernel corn
1 cup	lima beans
1 cup	green beans
2 stalks	celery, diced
2	carrots, diced
¼ cup	chopped parsley
	water
2 tbsp.	mustard
	salt to taste
2 tbsp.	Old Bay Seasoning to taste

Combine crab meat, water and Old Bay Seasoning. Simmer about 30 minutes. Add remaining seasonings and vegetables and simmer until vegetables are tender. Serves: Ten.

Steamboat Landing Rockfish

2 cups	cranberry juice
1	bay leaf
1 oz.	chopped celery
1 oz.	chopped carrots
2 ozs.	chopped onions
½ tsp.	corn starch
½ tsp.	water
1 tsp.	sugar
8 oz.	rockfish filet, deboned, scaled, skin left on
	salt and pepper to taste
	chopped parsley for garnish
6 oz.	jiccama, skin off, cut batonnet style
	vegetable oil for frying
6	dried cranberries, sautéed in sugar and butter, deglazed with 2 ounces of brandy, flambé, reduce liquid to syrup

Combine in a pot the cranberry juice, bay leaf, celery, carrots, and onions. Reduce to a ¼ cup. Combine the corn starch, sugar, and water. Add to the reduced cranberry juice to thicken slightly. Simmer for 5 to 10 minutes to cook out the corn starch. Set aside. Fry the jiccama in the vegetable oil and drain on a paper towel. Sprinkle with sugar. Set aside. Sauté the rockfish filet in clarified butter until done. Heat the sauce and mount with 1 tablespoon whole butter. Place the fried jiccama in the center of the plate as high of a pile as possible. Pour the sauce around the jiccama. Place the cranberries around the sauce. Put the rockfish on top of the jiccama. Garnish the rim of the plate with parsley. Garnish the rockfish with scallions cut on the bias. Serves: Two.

Steamboat Landing Restaurant

Index

Acknowledgments

Susie Armstrong Wills, Executive Editor

Denise McDonald, Cover Design

Mike Durham, Interior Text Design

Tab Distributing Company

Michael F. Trawick, Scans & Placement

Ken Kidd, K•R•K Typography

Robin Quinn, Copy Editing

Sue Knopf, Layout & Map Making

Louise Jennings, Copy Editing

José Garnham

Dean Gore

Pat Piper

Raymond McAlwee

Tom Vernon

PGSI/Printing & Graphic Services, Inc.

Photograph by Susie Armstrong Wills

Other Books by the Author

The Official Crab Eater's Guide
Chesapeake Bay Seafood Dining Guide
The Crab Cookbook
The Flavor of the Chesapeake Bay Cookbook
Baytripper Travel Guide, Volume I, Eastern Shore
Baytripper Travel Guide, Volume II, Western Shore

For ordering information and discount schedules:
Marian Hartnett Press, Box 88, Crisfield, MD 21817